PRAISE FOR HO̶̶ ̶̶ ̶̶ ̶̶SEXY

"Nillin's warmth, humor, and adventurousness are a shining light in the sex writing community. They live their queer, pervy life proudly, and in doing so, inspire others to be truer to themselves too. Reading their work serves as a wonderful reminder that sex is best when infused with fun, freedom, self-knowledge and self-expression."
—Kate Sloan, author of *101 Kinky Things Even You Can Do*

"Nillin's work in the sex blogging community has that magical quality of being both hot and filthy, and educating and thought-provoking. They are one of the most authentic sex bloggers I have ever had the pleasure of reading. They share their joys and their hardships with equal honesty and bravery. Their work is truly a celebration of queer love and sex."
—Molly Moore, creator of Molly's Daily Kiss and author of *Molly's Daily Kiss: Submission Of Truth*

"Mx. Nillin is a truly thoughtful writer whose work is always informative, frequently moving and often incredibly hot. Their sex blog is one of the best—they weave personal experience with education and advocacy so beautifully. Nillin's work is sorely needed in a world where sex and pleasure is still seen in deeply reductive, binary ways. With their welcoming approach and ability to knit honesty and vulnerability with education, I can think of few better guides through the landscape of 'sexy' than Nillin!"
—Girl on the Net

HOW DO I
SEXY?

ALSO FROM THE AUTHOR

Edited by Mx. Nillin Lore
Heckin' Lewd: Trans and Non-Binary Erotica

HOW DO I SEXY?

A GUIDE FOR TRANS AND NONBINARY QUEERS

MX. NILLIN LORE

FOREWORD BY SOPHIE LABELLE

THORNAPPLE
PRESS

How Do I Sexy?
A Guide for Trans and Nonbinary Queers

Thornapple Press
300 – 722 Cormorant Street
Victoria, BC V8W 1P8 Canada
press@thornapplepress.ca

Our business offices are located on the traditional, ancestral and unceded territories of the lək̓ʷəŋən and W̱SÁNEĆ peoples. We return a percentage of company profits to the original stewards of this land through South Island Reciprocity Trust.

Thornapple Press is a brand of Talk Science to Me Communications Inc. Talk Science is a WBE Canada Certified Women Business Enterprise, a CGLCC Certified 2SLGBTQI+-owned business, and a Certified Living Wage Employer.

Cover design by Sophie Labelle
Interior design by Jeff Werner
Substantive editing by Andrea Zanin
Copy-editing by Heather van der Hoop
Proofreading by Alison Whyte

Library and Archives Canada Cataloguing in Publication

Title: How do I sexy? :
a guide for trans and nonbinary queers / Mx. Nillin Lore.
Names: Lore, Nillin, author.
Description: Includes index.
Identifiers: Canadiana (print) 20240315286 | Canadiana (ebook) 20240315340 | ISBN 9781990869532 (softcover) | ISBN 9781990869549 (epub)
Subjects: LCSH: Transgender people—Sexual behavior. | LCSH: Gender-nonconforming people—Sexual behavior.
Classification: LCC HQ77.94.S48 L67 2024 | DDC 306.77086/7—dc23

10 9 8 7 6 5 4 3 2 1

Printed and bound in Canada.

MIX
Paper from responsible sources
FSC® C103567

*To all of the unforgettable trans and
nonbinary queers in my life. Be we partners,
lovers, friends or peers, this is for you.*

"Can't you just see it? Don't dream it, be it."
Dr. Frank-N-Furter, Rocky Horror Picture Show

CONTENTS

CONTENTS

FOREWORD

I still have vivid memories of that day in eighth grade when our sex ed teacher was finally going to talk about the "LGBT" chapter of the curriculum. It was 2002, and I was perceived as an artsy, effeminate, chubby boy obsessed with musicals. Everyone in the classroom knew that I had a closet full of dresses at home and that I fancied boys, and I was utterly desperate for some validation or confirmation that I, in fact, existed. My sexuality was the subject of countless rumours, ranging from an absence of genitalia (?!?) to actually being a trans boy (because I was secretly "really a girl"—I was just very bad at hiding it).

I stopped by the town library a few times a week on a never-ending quest to find representation or proof that I was allowed to dream myself a future. I spent whole evenings flipping through books, hoping to find characters who resembled me. Needless to say, I had read our sexual education textbook's chapter about LGBT people in advance. I waited in anticipation for days, envisioning this glorious moment when my classmates would be faced with the fact that people like me were worthy of dignity and recognition.

When that day came, our teacher first showed us a short film about HIV and the importance of protected sex. She said a few words about lesbian and gay people. There was another staff member who was openly bisexual, so we talked a bit about her. Then our teacher had this very memorable quote about trans people: "Let's skip this part about transsexuals, it's a bit too weird for me." And that was it. The whole thing must have lasted a whole nine minutes. We went back to our regular program of putting condoms on wooden dildos.

The worst part about this anecdote is that I still consider myself lucky that our teacher could even mention "LGBT people" without losing her job. Twenty-odd years later, it's not certain that she would have been able to do that. We just have to look at what's happening in different parts of Canada or the United States, where some conservatives are attempting to ban any mention of queer or trans people in schools, to realize that we can't afford to take our rights for granted. Heck, simply to have been able to attend a somehow sex-positive but heterosexist sex ed class feels like a privilege nowadays.

In this context, for queer, trans or gender-nonconforming people, finding confidence in inhabiting our meat vessels can be a lifelong journey. Circumstances such as social reprobation, minority stress, bullying, structural inequalities and intersectional considerations, to name a few, build up to create obstacles on the path to self-love. When we are told from an early age all the ways in which people like us are unlovable, we can only approach sexiness with feelings of doubt and inadequacy. At that point in my life, I avoided mirrors for weeks at a time, because I couldn't bear to see that shameful face of mine.

I think those obstacles explain why, more than 20 years later, I still feel echoes of the euphoria I experienced a few months after this disastrous sex ed class, when my soon-to-be boyfriend and I kissed for the first time. We went for a walk after watching the (quite transphobic, honestly) musical *Chicago* starring Renée Zellweger and Catherine Zeta-Jones at my grandmother's house. We were not done discussing the "Cell Block Tango" (we're still not over it, to be honest) when we kissed. It was –15°C and we were so cold and shivering that we kept hitting our teeth together. But I didn't care—it was the best day of my life. It unlocked a radical idea in me: despite everything that society always told me, I too could be desirable, and I didn't need to give up any part of myself in the process.

Feeling seen is something so powerful for trans, queer and gender-nonconforming people. You spend years or decades pretending, dressing up as someone you think people need you to be, putting on a show, only to realize that you're losing sight of who you truly are. When you quit playing this game, it's a puzzle to find out the things that are actually part of who you are, and that aren't simply there for the enjoyment of others. This part of exploration can be a great deal of fun, but it can also be scary and daunting.

That's why Mx. Nillin Lore's *How do I Sexy?* is so necessary. A book that takes the reader's hand while exploring the many aspects of sexiness from a queer and trans perspective couldn't come at a better time. Through Lore's stories and anecdotes, we are given a space to ponder on our own experiences. And that part is essential, because as Lore highlights several times throughout the book, sexy is subjective, and it's yours to define.

How do I Sexy? participates in the celebration of trans, queer and gender-nonconforming bodies in a unique, personal and bold way. The subject is vast and ambitious, but Lore manages to leave us begging for more in the end. And that's a good thing, because ultimately, the discussion is just beginning.

Stay divine!

Sophie Labelle, cartoonist and
musical enthusiast, January 7, 2024

ACKNOWLEDGEMENTS

This book came together in large part thanks to the encouragement and understanding of my partners, Fenric and Verne. Even when I struggled to focus and came face to face with my deepest fears, insecurities and feelings of imposter syndrome, they talked me down and helped me through it all.

The support and guidance that I've received from my counsellor Iris Akbar has also been instrumental in the creation of this book. It is because of my sessions with him that I've not only found a strong sense of purpose as a writer, but been able to learn patience and self-compassion, and to discover the self-confidence I needed to write this book.

Speaking of writing, I get that from my mom. No matter how much others have pushed against my dreams to write books, she instilled in me a love of the craft and gifted me with all of the creativity that flowed through her. Thanks, Mom!

I'm also incredibly grateful to Sophie Labelle for her amazing cover design and wonderful foreword! I've been a huge fan of Sophie's since the early 2010s, when I was just beginning to come out, so this has been an exciting full-circle moment for me. It genuinely means so very much to have her involved in this project. Thank you, Sophie!

Then there's all of my wonderful and insightful peers who contributed to this book with their perspectives: Andrew Gurza, Georgina "Gigi" Kiersten, Jiz Lee, Kevin A. Patterson, MEd, Mx. Praxis Phanes, Chelsea Poe, Ignacio G. Hutía Xeiti Rivera, Kate Sloan, Kelvin Sparks, Courtney Trouble and Vanniall. Thank you so much, to each and every one of you, for sharing your journeys and experiences! A big shout-out to Pink and White Productions, too, for all of the photos from the *Crash Pad Series* that they allowed me to use in chapters 6 and 8, featuring consenting trans and nonbinary queer adult performers.

Finally, none of this would even exist if it weren't for the enthusiasm that Eve Rickert, Hazel Boydell and Thornapple Press have shown toward getting *How Do I Sexy?* published and into the hands of as many trans and nonbinary queer readers as possible. Not to forget Andrea Zanin and Heather van der Hoop for their substantial insight, encouragement and editing guidance. I feel this is a much stronger book because of it.

Thank you all for investing in me and this passion of mine! I never could have done this alone.

CHAPTER 1
THE VENTURA EFFECT

Like most everyone else on the planet, I've long struggled with my image, body, confidence, self-worth and overarching self-perception. For me, this struggle goes beyond just physical insecurity, as I've also had to contend with deep-seated fear and shame around my gender and sexuality for most of my life. I don't see myself represented at all in many aspects of society, which makes it exceedingly difficult to have a positive view of myself. It's very sad to feel like there is something off about your body and image because everything you have to compare yourself to is so opposite to how you exist.

I'm a **nonbinary**, short, fat, hairy, **queer** person. I have wavered between overweight and obese, according to doctors, since my late teens, and that's made it especially difficult for me to feel confident and affirmed about myself throughout my life. While I've been fortunate enough to enjoy numerous relationships, romances, flings and intimate connections over the years, it's often been surprising to me.

Why? Because—and this is gonna sound harsh—I have a lot of negative self-talk and I generally don't see myself as an attractive person. Most of the time I can't wrap my head around why so many others seem to have seen me that way.

There are probably less daunting and terrifying ways of working through my overwhelming insecurities in search of some real self-worth than by writing an entire book ranting about that process, but that's how I roll! I've always been one to do my self-reflection rather dramatically and publicly—hence the decade's worth of deeply intimate content highlighting my successes, failures, relationships, heartbreaks, pleasures, lessons and more, with a sprinkle of hundreds of nudes, that I've been sharing on my very not-safe-for-work (**NSFW**) sex blog since the early 2010s.

Getting to this point was an incredibly arduous task. Yet despite all of that work, and the immensely affirming and equally queer community I built along the way, I still find myself lacking resources, guidance and positive representation of how a person like me might begin finding comfort and confidence in their body. Not that the internet is devoid of such representation, but what I have managed to glean has been buried deep in an ocean of **cisnormative**, **heteronormative**, fatphobic and misogynistic standards, ideals and expectations.

I have never had even a basic road map to guide my coming out and subsequent transition. No advertisements catered to me, or offered any products or services for queers like me. No films, television shows or magazines showed me any diverse bodies or identities in which I could find inspiration for myself. And pornography rarely depicted people like me as anything other than sexual oddities and "experiences" for **cis** people to have…at least if you're slim and "pass" enough, that is…which I am not, and don't. This is still the case, though it has been getting better in recent years as more independent creators put out radically affirming content, and a handful of larger production companies make a concerted effort to employ more diverse performers.

Nearly every morning, I struggle to dress myself because not only do most items of clothing not fit my body right, but few styles or brands seem to care about larger bodies. It's extremely difficult to feel attractive, sexy or even good in yourself when you have little to wear that's complementary, comfortable and euphoric. Then add in the fact that I don't often get to see queers like me depicted as being employable, enjoyable, lovable or happy. I don't get to see queers like me shown as desirable, popular or even social.

And so, I've spent most of my life so far searching for the one answer that's continued to elude me: how the fuck do I sexy? Seriously. How do I, Nillin Lore, sexy? How do I *feel* sexy? How do I *look* sexy? How do I *sound* sexy? How do I find emotional, romantic and sexual satisfaction in this world, in this body, with so little out there to encourage me?

More broadly, though, how can trans queer folk feel proud and excited about their identities, bodies and relationships when they still have to hide them in so many facets of their lives? How can they push back against all of the negative, fearful and othering discussion of their existence and forge satisfying and enriching lives?

Sure, I could just say fuck it, do my own thing and ideally attract the kind of partners I'm looking for, but that's easier said than done in a world that often dehumanizes or admonishes—and sometimes even outright demonizes—queer bodies and relationships. Not to mention the lifetime of negative reinforcement, self-doubt and internalized shame that still needs unpacking too.

I may not be able to change society with this book. But if you're reading it because you're looking for affirmations, resources and some guidance on how you can learn to express and explore yourself a little more, and maybe find some love and pleasure while you're at it, I hope something in here resonates for you.

No matter where you are on your journey, this book is for you.

ABOUT MY APPROACH

As much as I want this book to be accessible to as many people as possible, I have written it specifically for trans and nonbinary queer individuals, and therefore I assume readers have at least an intermediate understanding of the language, experiences and culture surrounding lesbian, gay, bisexual, trans, queer and other members of the sexual and gender-diverse community (**LGBTQ+**). I will not stop within the text to define queer terminology and concepts; however, you can find some definitions in the glossary included at the end of the book. (Words in the glossary are indicated in bold the first time they each come up in the text.) Still, I would like to address a couple of key points before continuing, as not everybody has the same perspective on the usage of certain words within our community.

When I write about trans people in this book, I am referring not just to trans women and trans men, but to all individuals who identify in any way as being **transgender**, **gender nonconforming** or even just not **cisgender**. This broad category includes people who are nonbinary, **gender-queer**, **agender**, **genderfluid**, **demigender**, **ambigender** and **neutrois**, as well as **crossdressers**, **traps**, **femboys**, **sissies**, **queens** and **kings**, should they consider themselves part of the greater trans, nonbinary and gender-nonconforming umbrella.

When I write about queer people in this book, I am referring to those who self-identify as queer, and I do not mean to apply this word to anyone who doesn't like it. Queer, to me, encompasses the broad and diverse range of sexual and emotional desires, attractions and relationships that exist outside of heterosexuality and traditional social norms. Referring to myself as queer encompasses both my sexuality and gender identity, as well as the myriad diverse ways I experience these identities socially, emotionally, romantically, physically and sexually. While it's typically used as an umbrella term, I use queer to describe myself as an individual who is neither cisgender nor heterosexual, and whose relationships exist outside of traditional structures and expectations.

When I say trans queer, I am referring to people who identify as trans or gender nonconforming, or otherwise not cisgender, as well as queer. And I hope trans queer people find this book helpful, because we have so few to look to that have been written specifically for us.

Next, I'm going to explain more of the "why" of this book and take a deep dive into the Ventura Effect I mentioned in the chapter title: what it is, what societal systems have contributed to it and how it remains harmful to us trans queers.

In chapter 2, we'll get right into defining and understanding what "sexy" means to various trans and nonbinary queer activists, advocates, creators and educators in contrast with how Western society generally approaches it. If you'd rather move on to the more practical pieces, chapters 3 and 4 deal with self-compassion and self-care for trans queers looking to heal their fears and insecurities. Chapter 5 focuses on unpacking and challenging a lot of the social systems and cultural programming that trans and nonbinary queers often have to face throughout their lives. Finally, in chapter 6 and beyond, we'll explore ways that you can start feeling sexy and discuss how to make intimate connections and find community, how to better understand your attractions and desires, and how to ensure that the sex and pleasure you experience is as affirming and enjoyable as it can possibly be.

There's no right or wrong way to read this book, so please read it in whatever order works best for you!

HOW "REPRESENTATION" IN FILM KEPT ME IN MY CLOSET

I've always fancied myself a pretty big nerd. Throughout my life, I've been a proud film buff (and Marvel Cinematic Universe know-it-all), an avid collector of comics and figurines and an obsessive gamer who has poured thousands of hours into both online and offline role-playing games.

Movies and television were always closest to my heart, though—so much so that I graduated from the University of Alberta with a major in film studies and had planned to then study at the Vancouver Film School before I had a change of heart. The movies and shows I watched growing up played an integral part in how I perceived myself and the world around me, and I desperately wanted to be a part of that magical storytelling.

It's too bad that, in retrospect, the vast majority of content I saw while growing up kept me in the closet until I was 26.

One of my earliest experiences with seeing trans representation of any kind was, unfortunately, the 1994 film *Ace Ventura: Pet Detective*. For those unfamiliar, the movie follows Jim Carrey, playing the titular Ace Ventura, as he investigates the theft of the Miami Dolphins's real dolphin mascot, as well as their missing star quarterback, just before the Super Bowl. It's a pretty simple plot, and being a big fan of Jim Carrey at the time, I expected I'd love this movie as much as his others. But it actually made me feel deeply uncomfortable and severely anxious about myself. About halfway through the film, Ace discovers that the kidnapper is a trans woman whom he had previously kissed. He becomes mortified and begins gagging, dry heaving, brushing his teeth, crying, and trying to induce vomiting in sheer disgust over the revelation. The message being sent was clear: trans women are deceptive, they transition with criminal intent, and the thought of kissing somebody who is trans should make anyone sick.

To drive this point home, the movie ends with Ace showing "proof" of his discovery by literally stripping this character down to her bra and panties in front of all of her coworkers before spinning her around to reveal the head of her tucked penis poking out from between the backs of her legs against her tight panties. As if this whole spectacle wasn't horrifically transphobic enough, Jim Carrey and the numerous police officers on screen then spend even more screen time gagging and projectile vomiting in response.

That hit me hard—especially since it was around the time when I had started to explore wearing my sister's skirts and dresses in secret whenever I had the chance. A few years prior, I had had my first kiss with my childhood friend, a boy I'd grown up with, who had me role-play as "the girl" while we explored our sexuality together. This was a huge catalyst for my self-perception and I was just beginning to take bolder and bolder steps in defining myself.

I remember that my friends cringed, groaned and laughed at Jim Carrey's revulsion toward the trans woman. They shook their heads, fake gagged and let out a chorus of "yuck," "gross" and "disgusting" as I sat there shivering, scared and ashamed, forcing myself to put on the same performance right alongside them.

Those reactions from people I cared about, and who supposedly cared about me, showed me that I needed to be doing a lot more to reject any sign of queer sexuality or gender nonconformity within myself if I wanted to be accepted. I thought something was deeply wrong with me. So I put myself into a closet, bolted it shut, boarded it up and padlocked chains around it, then threw the key into a deep, dark void.

Ultimately, I didn't come out for another 16 years.

I often refer to this impact as the Ventura Effect, which for me represented the fear, shame, stigma and extremely painful experience of internalized homophobia and **transphobia** that shaped my youth and formative teen years. The messaging I received from that film was then bolstered repeatedly throughout my life by even more movies and shows. These dehumanizing and degrading jabs directly contribute to, and maintain, a cultural environment that continues to make life hard for **gender-diverse** and sexually diverse folks—especially those who also experience further stigmatization and oppression under systems of racism and **ableism**.

After seeing the end of *Ace Ventura: Pet Detective*, I was genuinely terrified of the very idea of trans people. Similar transphobic content in the shows I grew up watching, such as *Family Guy* and *South Park*, only further cemented my anxieties around queerness. And you know who else was influenced by all that? All of my classmates and peers in elementary school, junior high and high school, all the way to college and university. The sheer onslaught of queerphobic jokes and insults that were thrown around schoolyards, classrooms and extracurricular activities was truly suffocating. All of this prejudice was often further entrenched by queerphobic parents, teachers, community leaders and figures, celebrities, politicians and more.

Then the internet and social media happened.

Not only was **queerphobia** and transphobia rampant in my day-to-day life while growing up, but everywhere I looked online was full of more and more prejudice toward trans and queer identities. A common warning I still hear today is to "never, ever read the comments" on literally any article or news story about queer and trans people. It's for good reason too. Go take a peek at any major piece about us on social media and you'll see an onslaught of terrible comments. Everyday conservatives bemoan "**snowflakes**," "politically correct (PC) culture" and "leftist censorship" while they actively **misgender**, **deadname** and dehumanize trans people with no repercussions whatsoever. **TERF**s call for lawmakers to ban us from public places, "concerned parents" rant about their kids being indoctrinated and "turned queer," and violent bigots make brazen and menacing comments about how they'd hurt, maim or kill us if they ever felt we were a threat to their daughters and wives.

Fact is, shit like the transphobia in *Ace Ventura: Pet Detective* is not "harmless fun" or "just a joke," because society does not operate in a vacuum and bigotry festers where it is normalized and forgiven. That movie is one pop-culture cog in a massive social machine that operates to reinforce a core tenet of Western society: trans people are gross and queers are a joke, whereas cisgender men and women in monogamous heterosexual relationships are normal and desirable.

For some of us, living in this cultural environment may mean a lifetime of misgendering, bullying, abandonment, and discrimination in education, employment and housing, as well as semi-regular street harassment. For others, it may mean being violently assaulted or even murdered by a family member, a group of drunken strangers or a prospective suitor who becomes repulsed and filled with shame upon learning that they were romantically or sexually pursuing a trans queer person.[1]

---

1 Alexandra Holden, "The Gay/Trans Panic Defense: What It Is, and How to End It," American Bar Association, March 31, 2020. https://www.americanbar.org/groups/crsj/publications/member-features/gay-trans-panic-defense/.

Each year, on Transgender Day of Remembrance (Nov. 20), our community mourns those of us who died as a result of transphobia and transphobic violence. We do our best, but we also struggle to truly know how many trans people are murdered annually because police services and the news media continue to misgender and deadname trans victims. The Trans Murder Monitoring report has managed to record well over 4,000 hate killings of trans people since January 2008,[2] and the vast majority of victims were Black and migrant trans women of colour, as well as trans sex workers. We'll also never know how many individuals die by suicide as a result of the transphobic prejudice, hatred, abuse, harassment and violence they face for being trans, nonbinary or gender nonconforming.

AND THEN THERE'S THE PORN...

As if all of that wasn't already enough of a hurdle, once I discovered pornography, all of the bad things about trans queer representation that I had seen in other forms of media got aggressively worse. While trans and gender-nonconforming people weren't necessarily ignored or erased (though they definitely were at times), they were instead fetishized, dehumanized and presented as a curious

---

2 Transgender Europe, "TVT TMM Update: Trans Day of Remembrance 2021." https://transrespect.org/en/tmm-update-tdor-2021/.

experiment, or a taboo prop or toy for **cishet** men and women to use and exploit for their own pleasure.[3]

Seeing trans people in this context was weird and confusing for me as a younger person. While they were shown to be more desirable in some ways, trans people were still referred to by slurs, and most of the content on major **tube sites** was super degrading and dehumanizing. Videos were mostly focused on trans women and showed them as toys for cis men, both straight and queer, to simply fuck and discard as they pleased. Other videos showed trans women as props for cis couples to use in "kinky" threesomes as a special "treat" that the husband could enjoy, or as experimental fucks for straight men to use to explore their queerness in a way they perceived as less threatening to their heterosexuality.

Gender nonconformity, while also present, was mostly shown in demeaning ways. The vast majority of these videos centred men in forced **feminization** and **sissification** scenarios wherein the crossdressing was done against their will for their wives's kinky appetites or, alternatively, for their own degradation kink. In both cases, the men faced a series of slurs, putdowns and vicious questions about their masculinity for even entertaining the idea of "dressing up."

Through it all, I didn't once see scenes in which any trans performers had their sexual pleasure and autonomy centred. Which is a damn shame, because a great deal of those erotic films had the potential to be empowering and enlightening,

---

3   Jes Grobman, "The Radical Potential of Trans Kink Porn," *The Establishment*, March 2, 2017. https://theestablishment.co/the-radical-potential-of-trans-kink-porn-cc6396773fd7/.

while simultaneously retaining the excitement and curiosity that likely drew many viewers to them.

It wasn't until my late twenties that I saw anything centring trans queer pleasure, and then it took me until my early thirties to find content that presented gender-diverse people as desirable, lovable and sexy. And so, as a gender-nonconforming queer, I couldn't see myself in those ways for most of my life either.

While it's bad enough for viewers consuming transphobic content, it's a lot worse for many individuals working in the industry. An interview I conducted with adult content creator Mx. Praxis Phanes on my blog back in 2018 offered me a glimpse at how it feels for those on camera. When talking about porn site categories and the terminology they use, Phanes was quick to highlight the hurt much of it causes: "A lot of trans women may be really put off or even hurt by kinks like sissification/feminization and humiliation because the last thing they want to feel is shame for being feminine."[4]

Further, adult filmmakers often have misinformed and unrealistic expectations of trans performers. "Another issue I see in shoots is producers expecting all **pre-op** trans women's penises to either be harder than they are, ejaculate, or other things that hormones hinder in a lot of instances," ey explained.[5]

---

4 Mx. Nillin Lore, "Talking Enby Visibility and Queer Inclusivity in Porn with Mx Praxis Phanes," MxNillin.com, October 11, 2018. https://mxnillin.com/mx-praxis-phanes-interview/.

5 Lore, "Talking Enby Visibility and Queer Inclusivity in Porn."

Phanes also mentioned how misunderstandings about diverse gender identities often result in harmful stereotypes, while also reducing employment opportunities for nonbinary and gender-diverse folks such as **emself**:

> Trans categories on clip and **cam sites** tend to be reserved for transitioning trans **folx**, specifically post-hormone/pre-op trans men and women. Whereas I understand this as a "niche" or "**fetish**" when it comes to sex work, it's frustrating for me as a nonbinary individual because if I put myself in the "trans" category (when camming for instance), I'll have members expecting something much different from a "**femme**"-looking person such as myself. Thus, I'm forced to put myself in the "female" category, which causes me to be misgendered a lot.[6]

It wasn't exactly clear to me all of those years ago, but through conversations like these and reading works from other sex-positive activists such as Jiz Lee, Chelsea Poe, Tobi Hill-Meyer and Sinclair Sexsmith, I now know that most of the early videos I had seen weren't meant to promote inclusion or respectfully showcase diverse genders and sexualities in any considerate or meaningful way. Rather, they were blatantly queerphobic, transphobic and fetishizing, and they were made for cishet viewers. They weren't made with trans people in mind, and they certainly didn't value the input or feelings of performers like Phanes.

---

6 Lore, "Talking Enby Visibility and Queer Inclusivity in Porn."

By the time I was in my twenties, two conflicting sets of beliefs were instilled in me, thanks to Hollywood and mainstream porn: (1) trans people are a joke and are dangerous, and being attracted to them means there's something wrong with you. But also, (2) they are sexy and fun for super-secret unique intimate experiences that we don't ever publicly admit to enjoying.

WHERE DO WE GO FROM HERE?

I leave you now with a quote from the Netflix documentary *Disclosure* (2020), which I highly recommend, as it presents trans voices from the film industry as they discuss their own experiences of the impacts of trans visibility in popular media, just as I have throughout this chapter. In the film, actress Jen Richards described a TV moment that had a profound impact on her, in which a father expressed unconditional love and support for his trans child. She then asked:

> *Why couldn't my mom have been like him? Why couldn't my friends have been like him and seen the value in my experience? But the person who's most responsible for failing to have that kind of vision is me. I have never seen myself the way that father saw his own child. I'd never seen myself that way. I'd never looked at myself with the kind of love and respect and awe that that father had for his own child. No one's looked at me that way. How could I*

*look at me that way? I had to see it. And now that
I have, I want that.*

I don't know about you, but I also want that. More than convincing anyone around me that I'm desirable, lovable and worthwhile, I want to convince myself. I know I'm not alone in this feeling. So that's exactly what we're going to do in this book! Through unpacking guilt and shame, developing positive self-care techniques, challenging your negative self-perceptions, looking at practical steps you can take to express your sexual self and exploring how trans queer–affirming sex can look for you, you'll be finding out what makes you feel sexy in no time!

CHAPTER 2
WHAT THE HECK EVEN IS "SEXY"?

How we each define "sexy" is subjective. However, I think it's also important to acknowledge that try as we might, the ways in which society frames sexiness has a huge bearing on our attractions to others and on our perceptions of ourselves as desirable sexual beings. This is why I adamantly encourage most trans queers who express anxiety or shame about their intimate selves to seek out community away from predominantly cisgender and heterosexual spaces.

There are simply big cultural differences between cishet society and trans queer communities, and finding community spaces away from heavily cisnormative and heteronormative environments can play a massive role in helping you understand and accept yourself. These spaces give you more opportunities to see other trans queers in affirming and positive ways and can contribute toward helping you see trans queer people as hot, attractive or alluring—all things that are excluded quite explicitly within cishet society as a whole.

After navigating my own coming out and meeting more trans queers, I'm confident in saying that I am almost exclusively attracted to visible queerness and overall gayness in others! It's that sweet, sweet gayness and gender nonconformity that gets me. The more trans queer somebody presents in terms of their gender expression, the more radical their hair, the more piercings and tattoos they have, the more nonconforming their presentation, the sexier I find them. The vast majority of my partners have been on the masculine end of the spectrum, self-identifying as **FTM**, **trans masc**, genderqueer, genderfluid or nonbinary trans men. To me, nothing's hotter than a cute, gender-nonconforming trans queer boy or **enby**.

I also find butts sexy! So, there's that too.

But my attraction to others isn't confined to just one wheelhouse. Over the years, I've also been involved with queer cis women and men, trans women, **androgynous** folks and crossdressers. Meanwhile, the porn and erotica I consume most is by far the kind featuring femboys. Femboy **furries**, to be exact. What can I say? I know what I like!

More important than appearance, for me, are qualities like authenticity, honesty and radically open vulnerability. Folks who embrace themselves while clearly and excitedly communicating their needs, wants and desires are attractive as all hell to me. When I'm first getting to know somebody, I don't want any of that small talk, either! I want to know about their interests, critical perspectives of the world, trauma relatability and everything that makes them feel awesome.

So, what I find sexy, though it's entirely queer, is actually pretty broad—as is what makes me feel sexy! I feel most physically attractive and confident when my beard is trimmed and shaped, my hair is styled in a sidecut and dyed purple or pink, and my outfit includes some cute leggings, a flowy skirt, and a nice, comfy top. In the bedroom, I feel sexiest in a leather chest harness, a comfortable jockstrap that makes my package look nice and plump, and sometimes, a collar on my neck and a **pup hood** over my head.

I've also recently come to realize just how impactful my social transition has been in regard to feeling sexy. I've always felt a little weird about my transition, like I couldn't do much to address the **dysphoria** that I experience. Being a nonbinary, gender-nonconforming person means that my experiences with my body, with my self-perception, can be complicated, and it makes transitioning a lot more challenging. It also makes my experiences with dysphoria harder to quantify and treat because some social aspects of both masculinity and femininity work for me, while others do not, and my relationship with my physical body is often quite complex. The truth is that in an ideal world I would have been assigned female at birth (**AFAB**) and then transitioned as trans masc or a trans man. But that's not something that any form of social, surgical or medical transition can help me with, and I don't feel that it is entirely accurate to define myself as being a trans man, even if that is how I see and experience myself. Interestingly, this personal revelation suggests to me that regardless of how I was born, and how my body was labeled, I would be trans. It's sad to me that there's no feasible road to transitioning how I truly wish I could, but I've found a lot of solace and comfort in gender nonconformity and in embracing both my body and my queer masculinity on my own terms.

So far, a lot of my growth and changes have been based around my name, pronouns, clothing and overall embracing my authentic queer self. That means not trying to deepen my voice or stifle any of my "softer" mannerisms, and not worrying that how I'm sitting—or standing, or acting, or sounding—is "too queer." All of that felt like it was expected of me at one point or another, and it was a lot to deal with. Ultimately, deciding that I had no interest in striving to "pass" as any particular gender, and that I did not want any form of medical or surgical transition for myself, was immensely liberating.

That freedom has led to a lot of surprises about what makes me feel hot. For example, as a belated Christmas 2022 gift, my husband Fenric got me a nose bridge piercing and it immediately changed how I saw myself for the better. Not only did the piercing feel incredibly complementary, and like it should have been there for years, but I've also felt infinitely cooler and sexier ever since I got it. It hadn't occurred to me that my piercings could be considered as part of my gender expression and transition, but hells yeah they can! Getting the bridge of my nose pierced helped me appreciate my other piercings even more (I have 2-gauge plugs in both of my ears, a bar in my right eyebrow, and snakebite piercings).

In sum: I'm a big gay trans queer who's into other super gay trans queers. That's what turns me on and makes me feel hot. But that's just my experience, and yours could differ a little, or wildly! There's no singular way that sexy has to work.

Which brings me to the most consistently frustrating questions I've struggled to concretely answer on my blog, in my presentations and through my self-advocacy efforts throughout the last couple of decades. Sexy: What the hell is it? How the hell do you do it? What does it freakin' feel like?

Honestly...after years of reading about, writing about and discussing these questions with others, I've come to realize that I don't entirely know how to answer them. But since you're here (thanks for buying my book!), let's take a crack at figuring out what the answers might be for you.

THE DICTIONARY DEFINITION

I personally like Merriam-Webster, so let's go with that. The online version of their dictionary defines sexy as:

1. sexually suggestive or stimulating: Erotic
2. generally attractive or interesting: Appealing

And that seems pretty on par with how other dictionaries, society and pop culture approach the word. The consensus is that "sexy" informally describes somebody, or something, that is interesting, appealing, alluring, sexually appealing, attractive or exciting.

Not very helpful, I know.

In fact, it makes nailing down what sexy is even harder! Especially for trans queer individuals, or members of any marginalized groups. In North America and the United Kingdom, and other Western-influenced cultures or colonized regions (which is a staggering proportion of the world), what we find depicted as sexy tends to be overwhelmingly white, cisgender, able-bodied, thin or fit, and within the context of monogamous heterosexuality.

Just look back to chapter 1 and think about how transphobia in popular culture and media feeds into transphobic societal sentiments that inform our worldviews. Then think about how often films and television shows present skewed, and highly specific, archetypes for what bodies and identities should be celebrated. These are the bodies of superheroes, action stars, love interests, explorers, outlaws, warriors and more—all unattainable and unrealistic, yet aggrandized for decades. And all are further framed by toxic gender roles, cisgender and heterosexual identity, privilege, violence and vanity.

It's no wonder so many of us have struggled with communication around our needs, as well as insecurities and negative self-perceptions. How could we not, when our expectations of ourselves, and our expectations of our partners, have been so heavily influenced by all of this imagery? Meanwhile, sexual desire and eroticism are far more complex and varied than what is typically modeled, and what most of us were taught.

A BROADER AND MORE INCLUSIVE APPROACH TO ATTRACTION

With all of this in mind, let's convolute things even more! If we're talking about sexuality, what makes us feel sexy, what attracts us and what we desire, long for and lust after, then we also have to talk a little about all of the other forms of attraction that you can experience. Because as we've already seen here, what's attractive to folks tends to be a big ball of gendy-bendy sexy-wexiness. And attraction tends to be based on a lot more than strictly a desire to fuck, or be fucked by, somebody.

First off, there's good old-fashioned sexual attraction. That's the one most people tend to think of when we discuss attraction. If you've ever looked at somebody and thought, "Damn, I want to see them naked" or "I wonder what their thighs would feel like around my head," or felt incredibly flushed, maybe even a little tingly in your nether regions, that would be sexual attraction.

You might think that physical attraction is the same thing, considering that so much of sexual attraction tends to be based on a desire for physical acts. However, in this case, we're talking more about sensuality. Whereas sexual attraction tends to lead us to want a lot of super-explicit stuff involving genitals, mouths and possibly buttholes, physical attraction can encompass a broad range of other needs and wants, such as cuddling, hugging, kissing, head rubs, massages and more. If you've ever wanted to snuggle up with somebody while watching your favourite TV shows, or to hold hands with a mega cutie while out on a walk, but not necessarily have that lead to anything else, you could have been experiencing physical attraction.

Aesthetic attraction is all about what you see and how that makes you feel. It happens a lot for folks who go through different scenes or get into fandoms of various kinds. For example, maybe you absolutely love everything about the look and vibe of goth queers, or punks, or **gender-fucking** femboys. You may be drawn to these people in a way that includes a desire to emulate their looks in your own life and presentation, or it could just be that any time you see these aesthetics in the wild, you start to uncontrollably sweat from excitement for the whole vibe. Either way, it's possible to be attracted or drawn to an aesthetic in general without feeling desire for the specific people you see presenting it.

Finally, we have romantic attraction. That tends to be where the lovey-dovey feels come from. Being romantically attracted involves actively wanting to date somebody with the intention for the relationship to include a mutual goal of developing emotional vulnerability, intimate connectivity and some degree of passionate, romantic love. Experiences of romantic attraction vary, but can include wanting to care for another person, contribute to their happiness and fulfillment, and establish a deep connection. Romance is a hard concept to pin down, but some definitions suggest that it's got an element of mystery and magic that sets it apart from other feelings of emotional attraction and connection. Romantic attraction often overlaps with other types of attraction, such as physical or sexual, but not always. For example, people in **queerplatonic relationships** enjoy deeply fulfilling partnered bonds that are emotionally invested, but do not always centre romantic or sexual acts and experiences.

All of that being said, there can be so much crossover between the types of attraction, and everyone's experience differs in ways that may make it confusing to suss out exactly how you're feeling about somebody. Do you love them? Do you want to fuck them? Do you want to be like them? Do you just want to hang out socially and cuddle? Or all of the above!? Bah! Feelings are complicated, and our attractions to others are too.

On top of it all, let's also consider the spectrum of **asexual** (ace) and **aromantic** (aro) folks. People who identify as asexual frequently report experiencing little sexual attraction to others, or even none at all, yet they can still be attracted to somebody emotionally, aesthetically or physically. Asexuality may look very different from one ace person to another. Some ace individuals may not want to have sex but may enjoy masturbating, either on their own or with a partner; other ace folks aren't interested in any sexual activity, whether with others or on their own. Some ace folks consent to having sex with a partner because they enjoy participating in their partner's experiences of pleasure, but have no personal desire for sex themselves. People who are aromantic experience little emotional attraction, or none at all, but they can still have strong sexual, physical or aesthetic desires. Despite not feeling romantic emotions for others, they may still be comfortable with doing things that a partner finds romantically fulfilling.

In practice, all of these different kinds of attraction can create a lot of variation in how you experience your desires and how you might consider approaching them. You can be sexually attracted to somebody but not feel any romantic desire, or any need for physical intimacy outside of sexy times. You can also want to cuddle somebody and hold their hand, but have no interest in pursuing anything sexual or forming any sort of committed bond. Heck, you can even just think somebody looks awesome, and maybe you think about them a lot and want to emulate their look, and that's all it ever is. Or you can feel a combination of all these attractions at once, or experience some of them really strongly now but not as much later on. It's all valid, it's all fluid and it all plays into how we feel attracted to others, and what makes us feel attractive to them.

Sadly, I don't have any grand revelations here to guide you toward sexy enlightenment, but what I do have is a ton of experience navigating all of these types of attraction and my overall desires over the last 20-odd years, plus a mountain of resources and tips to help you along your way.

We happen to be extremely lucky in that, in recent years, gender nonconformity and queerness have become significantly more visible in many areas, which means we have so much more to look at and talk about when we're trying to figure out what makes us feel most attractive and affirmed in ourselves. Between the internet allowing queer folks to reach larger audiences on social platforms, advertisements featuring more diverse models, and various films and television projects focusing on more than just cishet characters, it's arguably easier now than ever before to discover your own vibe, both in and out of the bedroom. Finding your sexy self often comes from a combination of your own self-perception mixed with inspiration from the world around you.

WHAT OTHER TRANS QUEERS FIND SEXY

I spoke earlier about the things I found most attractive in others. Now, I also want to share additional perspectives from some of the many amazing trans queers I've come to know and work with over the years. What I find most attractive and alluring isn't universal by any means, and I feel there's great value in seeing a range of unique desires from typically marginalized voices.

I wanted to ensure that the other perspectives I chose to share came from folks who were well versed in trans queer experiences and who held body- and sex-positive ideals. So I reached out to my fellow sex writers, bloggers, artists, adult entertainment performers and content creators, as well as activists and advocates. Some I've considered friends for years. Others, I've long wanted to connect with, and this project gave me a more concrete reason to work through my imposter syndrome and start that conversation. Regardless of how long I've known them, each person I spoke with had deeply insightful advice to share on the topic of sexiness.

For Andrew Gurza (they/he), an award-winning disabled, nonbinary disability awareness consultant living in Toronto, Canada, sexy is safe, respectful intimacy and closeness. They summarized it pretty well through sharing the ways their disability has informed their identity and experiences: "Part of my journey and realization that I am nonbinary was understanding that I was unable to engage in a lot of the physicality of gay male queerness. When someone is able to engage in deep conversation with me, and is willing to learn about my disabled experience and how that will impact our sexual relationship, I find that incredibly sexy. I am so proud that my disabled experiences have allowed me to shift what I find sexy."

Gurza's need for a potential partner, lover or **play friend** to show a vested interest in learning more about their disability, and communicating about how intimacy can look for them, deeply resonated with me. As an autistic person with pretty intense attention deficit hyperactivity disorder (**ADHD**) and complex post-traumatic stress disorder (**C-PTSD**), I also find that I feel safest and most invested in somebody when they ask me about those aspects of myself. The more that somebody wants to participate in open discussion about how to build an affirming space to be intimate together, the better I feel overall about being sexual and vulnerable with them.

Nonbinary porn performer Jiz Lee (they/them) is all about confidence when it comes to what they find sexy—not just in terms of how comfortable somebody is in their skin, but also in how clear and assertive they are about their needs, wants and boundaries. "It means being able to ask for help, to correct course, to receive 'no' in a way that affirms and respects everyone involved," they explained. "Confidence helps communication be open and honest, building trust. Now that's sexy!" This sentiment was echoed by my friend Kate Sloan (she/her), a sex journalist, podcaster and author of *101 Kinky Things Even You Can Do*, who said, "There is nothing inherently 'unchill' or embarrassing about admitting, 'I find you very cute and I get a little nervous around you!' and asking for whatever you think might ease those feelings: reassurance and compliments, cuddles, massage, non-goal-oriented kissing, etc."

Confidence is also sexy for Georgina "Gigi" Kiersten (they/them), a Black, asexual, queer trans author of diverse LGBTQ+ romance and erotica. In their case, as an asexual person, sexiness is more about aesthetics. Since they don't experience sexual attraction, they instead find that how someone carries themself is what draws them in: "I love a person who has a certain swagger to them. What attracts my attention is especially a **BIPOC** [Black, Indigenous or person of colour] person who can walk into any room and just own it. It is something that can transcend skin colour, body shape or gender."

From a more sexual perspective, confidence is extremely sexually attractive for Dutch American filmmaker and performer Chelsea Poe (she/her), whose performances have earned her five awards and many other nominations from prominent news organizations within the adult film industry such as XBiz and Adult Video News (AVN). Poe told me that while growing up, she struggled with understanding her sexuality because she never found herself attracted to any specific body types or physical attributes in others. Once she discovered **BDSM** imagery online, she had a major revelation and began to understand herself as a sexual being. Now she finds a dominating personality to be the most attractive characteristic in others, and kink has been immensely formative to her overall identity. Beyond this voyage of self-discovery, participating in BDSM has allowed her to experience intimacy with all sorts of people she possibly wouldn't have connected with otherwise: "I think my kink interests [are] what really make me identify with the term queer. In real life, I've basically only dated people who read to the world as women so I feel in many ways I've always been read as a lesbian, but with fetish/BDSM it really blurs the lines of who and what I'm attracted to."

While I'm personally more attracted to an adorably awkward, shy, clumsy trans queer who hides in their hoodie than I am a more bombastic or outgoing personality, I can absolutely see how confidence also plays a big part in what I find sexy. I think confidence is far more nuanced than outward expression or social performance. Being awkward, shy or even quiet doesn't necessarily mean a person lacks confidence or is unable to communicate effectively in the ways that are needed. Most of the awkward trans queers I've been intimate with may have stumbled quite cutely through flirting, and gotten their head stuck in their shirt or tripped before seductively crawling into bed, but when it came down to the important bits, they were able to directly communicate their desires, expectations and consent. And yeah, that is supremely sexy!

I also relate to what queer author and educator Kevin A. Patterson (he/him), MEd, told me was most sexy to him: "I'm always wary of overstepping. That's why enthusiasm is so sexy for me. Even if we can't find the availability to have fun, just knowing that there's an unambiguous interest in doing so is enough for me sometimes." I'm a very anxious person at the best of times and struggle with reading either too much, or too little, into people's body language, mannerisms and expressions. So the more excited and eager somebody is about spending time with me, or the experiences that we want to have together, the more into that connection and person I'm bound tb be.

I was moved by the definition of sexy shared by Ignacio G. Hutía Xeiti Rivera (they/elle), MA, founder and co-executive director of The HEAL Project. Elle drew attention to something that certainly resonates for me, which is all the little things that are often overlooked or minimized: "Sexy is the way somebody smiles, the way they express their gender, the shape of their nose, the curvature of their fupa, the junk in their trunk or the way that a word falls from their lips. All of those can get my initial attention. Draw me in and possibly flirt." A lot of that resonated with me because it's absolutely all those little things about somebody's queerness, gender expression, quirks and personality traits that also draw me in so heavily. Hence why I find myself constantly gravitating toward those trans masc queers who tell dad jokes, express their gender and queerness quite explicitly, rock a lot of 2000s goth and punk rock vibes, and still unironically do the finger guns.

Finally, I found it interesting how Kelvin Sparks (he/him), a **nonmonogamous**, bisexual trans man blogger and author, was most attracted to playing with the idea of desire. For him, this attraction is informed by the romance novels he read as a teenager about characters that really want each other but can't act on those desires. As an adult, his more **Dominant** fantasies focus heavily on giving a **submissive** what they desire but are unsure how to ask for. It's all about the anticipation for Sparks: "That buildup of longing, aching, yearning and the inevitable part where the tension finally lets loose is really erotic to me (and I even find tragic stories where the tension never breaks to be equally erotic, in an emotionally masochistic way)."

I personally struggle with stories where erotic tensions never come to fruition, but that tends to be in large part because of how often I feel frustrated that trans queer sex and romance is teased in a lot of mainstream content, yet never made explicit. While I understand that Sparks means denial can be just as erotic as all of the teasing, desperation and hope for pleasure and release, it's just not quite my thing. However, I wholeheartedly agree that the anticipation of building up to something intimate and exciting with another person is exhilarating. It's something I strive to do with my partners through foreplay and sexy private messages throughout the week, regardless of precisely when sexy times may occur.

WHAT MAKES OTHER TRANS QUEERS FEEL SEXY THEMSELVES

My peers expressed a broad range of perspectives about what they find appealing and erotic in others. When I asked what makes them personally feel sexy, they also shared a great diversity of ideas. Once upon a time, when I was in my early twenties, if I had asked my friends what made them feel sexy, either I'd have been met with ridicule for even bringing it up, or I'd have heard all about their desires to have typically idealized bodies and be with people who did too. I always felt huge anxiety when faced with so much focus on physical attributes being what made somebody sexy. As you might recall, I've always struggled with my body, and having doctors define me as overweight or obese made it difficult for me to feel sexy about my body at all—especially considering how often comedies, romance films and other pop culture media treat fat people as gross, ugly or a joke.

Again, it's truly uplifting to see that for many of the trans queers I know now, sexiness encompasses a spectrum of contributing factors, none of which seem to come in absolutes. The consensus seems to be that bodies come in all shapes and sizes, and they don't have to define our attractiveness. Feeling sexy can be about how others make you feel safe, respected, desired and heard. It can be about communication, creativity, experimentation and open-mindedness. And at its core, feeling sexy is all about knowing you can safely express your needs, wants, desires, sexuality, gender and overall identity in an empowering and affirming way. I feel that my peers reiterated this through our conversations.

Just as she said kink is a core part of how she experiences attraction and desire, Chelsea Poe also found it to be formative for her sexual self-perception. "I feel like what makes me feel sexy is feeling useful in a BDSM context," she explained. "I've always kind of had partners who were Dommes since I was 20 because I believe the root of my sexuality is really being a BDSM submissive."

Similarly, Kelvin Sparks has found that kink offers him the opportunity to further explore and assert his gender identity in enriching ways. "It feels very powerful to affirm myself as a top, especially as my status as a queer trans man means I'm usually assumed to be a bottom," he told me. "Working on my kinky topping skills makes me feel sexy. Whether it's rope or flogging or electroplay, feeling competent makes me feel confident."

Sparks is also quite invested in leather fetishism and explained to me that physically expressing himself in a way that feels sexy tends to involve leather clothing and accessories such as harnesses, strap-ons, boots, jackets and more. But for Sparks, wearing leather isn't just about feeling attractive; it also involves experiencing a sort of sacred connection with other queer leather wearers throughout history. "It feels like [leather accessories] connect me to other **butch** queer people (across time and space) in finding eroticism in them, whether that be butch **dykes** in work boots or leathermen at an **Eagle**."

I like that approach a lot, and I had never thought of it in connection to my own enjoyment of wearing pup hoods, chest harnesses, collars and other **pet play** items. One of the biggest things I've observed about pet play, especially when it comes to pups, is how so much of the online community and content generated by it seems dominated by trans and queer men. And not just one kind of trans or queer man, either. I see queer dudes—cis and trans, of a wide range of ages, with all sorts of body types—deeply enjoying and finding sexual pleasure, fulfillment and confidence in pup play. And when I wear my hood or other gear, I too sometimes experience a sense of belonging and connection to bygone days of early queer liberation that's hard for me to fully explain.

Georgina Kiersten had a harder time answering the question of what makes them feel sexy because being asexual meant they didn't relate to that experience. Instead, they understand the idea of feeling sexy as being similar to feeling confident and self-assured, and for them, that comes from having a brazen sense of style. "Wearing bright colours and patterns, having my makeup and accessories on point," they said. "For me, the more colourful and bold I am, the more confident I become."

Style is part of the picture for others too. Kate Sloan likes to take photos of her outfits for her blog and social media, and to look back on them later in search of trends around what tends to make her feel sexy and confident. "When I find myself returning to look at a selfie several times because the sight of it makes me feel affirmed, cute and desirable, that's usually a good clue that something I'm wearing in that photo—or something about the way I've done my hair or makeup—makes me feel sexy and could be brought into the bedroom if I ever wanted a confidence boost before or during sex," she noted.

As a sex blogger myself, I can relate to Sloan's point. Over the decade that I've been writing about my intimate sex life and personal journey, I've also posted a great number of selfies, cute outfit pics and full-on nudes of myself. Seeing people compliment me in the comments not only excites me and fulfills the exhibitionist in me, but also makes me feel incredibly desirable. It's a big positivity boost for me and helps offset the negative self-talk that usually bogs down my brain. And like Sloan, a lot of my current look, which makes me feel the most authentically me that I've ever felt, came from looking through all of my past photos. I also find myself going back to certain photos, or resharing them, many times. Paying attention to the finer details of what specifically makes me feel good about those images of myself goes a long way toward helping me cultivate a better, more cooperative relationship with my sexual self.

Courtney Trouble (they/she), a femme queer adult performer, indie porn maker, artist, poet and writer, is also a big fan of mixing fashion with sex. In fact, they believe this is why they enjoy being a porn star so much: "I love the chance to get all dolled up! I really love all kinds of lingerie, from stockings and garters to the clear vinyl bondage gear I get from Stockroom, or even a bra harness made out of rope ties, or thigh straps and a one-piece teddy," they explained. "I guess what I really love to do is make my bondage gear feel like an outfit by mixing it up with my lingerie and a cute hair and makeup look! It always feels like playtime once I've had the prep time."

Finally, Vanniall (she/they), a trans sex worker and content creator living in New York City, told me about how fragrance makes them feel sexiest: "Before I go anywhere, or even [when I'm] sitting on the couch at home, I'll make sure to spritz myself with my favourite smell and all of the sexy memories associated with that smell always come rushing back."

I'd never thought about how fragrance could make me feel sexy like that. Although, when I think about it, I've always had severe anxiety about smelling bad to my partners, which can make me feel very unsexy. In recent years, this anxiety has gotten a lot better, thanks in large part to my husband Fenric, who gets incredibly worked up about how good I smell and how horny it makes him. His desire for my natural odour can boost my confidence like nothing else at times, and truthfully, I can't get enough of how good he smells and how much it turns me on too. It's actually a pretty common kink called **olfactophilia**! And reading Vanniall's answer about fragrance and smell ended up helping me think about the sexiness of scent in a self-affirming way. A bottle of perfume may not do it for me, but when I smell Fenric's armpits, or hair, or body, it causes all the sexy memories associated with his scent to come rushing back. And hearing him growl in my ear, loudly whispering about how incredible I smell, definitely makes me feel sexy.

FIGURING OUT WHAT IT MEANS TO YOU

Now that you've heard what I find attractive and what makes me feel sexy and desirable, and you've heard similar thoughts from several other sex bloggers, authors and adult performers, it's time to think about yourself. In reflecting back on your life, your relationships, your intimate experiences and the people you've been drawn to, what do you see? Are there patterns in the type of folks you date? Are you particularly drawn to any specific identities? Do you find any specific traits, aesthetics or vibes attractive?

Having a good idea of what you find attractive in others can potentially help you discover what feels sexy for you personally. Do goth and emo styles get your motor running? Would that look also make you feel more attractive if you applied aspects of it to yourself in some contexts? Do you find clear communication, confidence and authenticity to be desirable traits in a potential partner? Are those things you'd also like to work on for yourself, to help you feel more self-assured?

Maybe you're realizing it's simply that you need some hot, complementary clothes and accessories that get you the attention you crave while also making you feel excited, aroused and poised. You just want to feel hot as fuck and turn some damn heads, maybe get the hookups you wish you were having. That's legit and it's absolutely an attainable goal! And hey, if you happen to be on the ace/aro spectrum, but still want to feel sexy or attractive, that's also valid and you deserve it, friend!

Even if you don't find yourself sexually attracted to much, perhaps others have styles and qualities that you find aesthetically attractive. Considering these styles and vibes can also help you find ideas for ways that you too can look and feel desirable in yourself, regardless of what your intentions may be. Because the truth is that feeling sexy doesn't have to be about sex at all! Plenty of us get dressed up to go to the club, or out shopping, with no intention of having intercourse with anyone, and getting dressed up to look hot and draw the attention of others is not an explicit invitation for sex. Many of us just want to feel desirable, with or without it leading to anything particularly sexual, and that's OK.

If you're still not quite sure about what it is that would make you feel sexy, don't worry. I've got you. But first, we've got some more introspection and self-reflection work to do!

CHAPTER 3

COPING WITH FEAR, SHAME, GUILT AND INSECURITY

~~~~~~

Content Note: this chapter discusses struggles with mental health, addictions, self-harm and unsafe sex practices.

~~~~~~

Sometimes it can be hard existing in this world as a trans or nonbinary queer. Between all the anti-trans activists and lobby groups, the bigoted policy development and lawmaking, the daily **microaggressions** and institutional oppression, it can be challenging to find the time, space or energy to truly celebrate yourself or centre positive personal growth. And even if you find yourself able to do so, it can be quite difficult to track down affirming resources for trans and nonbinary queers, created by members of our own community, that foster self-reflection and promote self-development. Everything tends to be just so...cishet.

I hope this book can help start filling some of these gaps for our community. I want it to be one of those affirming resources that you can confidently turn to as needed whenever you're feeling insecure, unsure of yourself or in need of an uplifting boost. But working to feel better can involve tackling some pretty intense feelings and experiences that tend to keep us in repeat patterns of doubt, fear and even self-denial.

Many of us, myself included, have gone through a lifetime of struggling with systems and social interactions that invalidate, other and sometimes even dehumanize people on the continuum of sexual and gender diversity—and that's when we're not just being ignored, forgotten about, or dismissed and excluded. As those experiences add up, they can deeply affect us. Maybe you've felt too afraid to fully come out, for fear of how your friends and loved ones may respond. Perhaps you've been exposed to many negative opinions, beliefs and jokes about trans and nonbinary queer folks, and you've internalized them to such a degree that you find it overwhelming and embarrassing to contemplate queerness in relation to yourself. Or maybe you were raised in an environment that guilts and shames individuals for having any sexual thoughts or desires whatsoever, let alone any that aren't strictly heterosexual, and that experience has made the notion of pursuing the connections you truly desire feel impossible.

I get that. I've been there too.

Or maybe you've already done a lot to work through difficult emotions in previous parts of your journey! Now those experiences are mostly resolved, or even just more peripheral, rather than directly impacting your self-perception in any major way. That's valid! If you find yourself feeling quite happy and content with where you're at, and not experiencing much fear, shame, guilt or other negative emotions about your identity and self-expression, you might want to skip ahead a little. You'll find the more practical advice and resources on sexual self-expression, dating, finding community and more in chapter 6 and beyond. You might still like to brush up on developing your mantras in chapter 4, which could help you establish your wants, desires, intentions and guiding principles along with some positive self-affirmations.

However, if you find that guilt, shame or fear instilled in you by society and your personal experiences is blocking you from finding your sexual self, feeling sexy and understanding your self-worth, then please keep reading! These next couple of chapters will help you challenge, unpack and ultimately start to heal from those experiences while you move forward with enthusiasm. I plan to guide you through some of this process first by telling my own story, and then by going over some of the more impactful intrusive thoughts and internal challenges that trans and nonbinary queers can face. Finally, I'll offer a number of detailed suggestions on how to begin moving yourself forward with compassion.

I also want to take a moment here to explicitly say that you're not going to magically overcome all of your past experiences in one go, and it's OK to still struggle with insecurity, anxiety, intrusive thoughts and trauma while working through the rest of this book. Focusing too much on trying to "fix" these things can become another hurdle in and of itself if you're too hell-bent on reaching some unrealistic standard or goal for your mental health and coping skills. While it's good to work through your emotions about past experiences, and take steps toward improving your relationship with yourself and how you see yourself, it's also important to keep moving forward as best you can even if some things still feel troublesome. You're still worthy of feeling sexy even if you're incredibly sad, unsure of yourself, unclear on your identity, or in the midst of unlearning and freeing yourself from the transphobic and queerphobic ideals that were instilled in you. It's OK to be at the beginning of your journey and to desire to connect with your sexual self right away.

So, let's get to it!

Let me start by sharing a bit of my own story so you know where I'm coming from.

THE BOY I MINIMIZED, INVALIDATED AND HID

It's both fitting and hilarious to me that my first kiss occurred in an actual closet. And it may sound a little cliché, but my journey, and the battle for my big gay soul, all started with the boy I kissed in that closet.

Let's call him Jett (to protect his identity, this isn't his real name). He had adorable curly brown hair and a cute smile, and whenever I was with him, I felt weirdly nervous and worried about what he thought of me. Our parents were all serving in the Canadian Armed Forces and Royal Canadian Air Force in Trenton, Ontario, so we quickly became childhood besties. At the time I wasn't aware that this was a crush, but looking back it's painfully obvious I was having a lot of big feelings for this boy.

I mean, how could I not? He was my first kiss, and he was so damn cute!

We both knew that we shouldn't have been doing what we were doing together. Things like making out, dry humping, being naked together and touching each other was stuff only adults should do. It was definitely not for us to be doing during sleepovers when we were sure everyone else had fallen asleep, or when our parents were too busy drinking and socializing to check in on us. But we did. We stayed up late to quietly explore and play in our dark bedrooms any time we had the opportunity. After a while it felt like a given that if we were having a sleepover, regardless of whose place it was at, we were going to be fooling around.

It's interesting that the word "sex" never came to mind during any of these experiences. We knew what sex was, but we were both boys, and boys didn't have sex with boys. Sex was something boys did with girls. Not that we even thought about the layers of it all that much. All we were concerned about was that it felt good, it was fun and we liked doing it together. Besides, we covered our bases on the whole gay thing because early on, when we first started making out in secret, we talked about it and decided that I was the girl and Jett was the boy.

Boom. Gayness avoided.

In hindsight, it saddens me that we so instinctually worked to dismiss the queerness of our connection by trying to make it "straight" through what was essentially role-playing as heterosexual. Even today, I wonder: if either of us had received a more comprehensive sex education that included queer sexualities and trans identities, would we have still done that? Would one of us have needed to "be the girl" in order for kissing to be OK? Would we have realized that stuff like mutual masturbation, dry humping, hand jobs and blow jobs were sex even when two boys were doing it? While I recall my friendship with Jett very fondly, I also think that it was in many ways the beginning of my internalized queerphobia. These were my first sexual experiences, my first queer experiences, and their foundation was built on invalidating that queerness in whatever ways we could.

I didn't understand the gravity of that perspective at the time.

Eventually, my dad was reposted to Ottawa and we moved nearly three hours away from Jett's family. Jett and I grew apart, but during the few times my family drove back to Trenton for a visit, it wasn't long before Jett or I suggested that we could "do that thing we used to," and the making out, cuddling and play commenced. When my parents retired in 1997 and moved the family across Canada to Edmonton, Alberta, that was the end of it all. I never saw Jett again. He'd pop up in my mind from time to time, but I didn't linger on those memories for long and never told anyone else about him.

Jett became so far removed from my mind that little details of what he looked like, and the experiences we had together, also started to fade. My choice to not talk about him and not think about him frequently had a lot to do with the Ventura Effect. The avoidance was almost reflexive after seeing the film and how my peers reacted. I just instinctively stopped remembering him, quickly pushed him out of my mind anytime he popped back in there, and instead focused on my new school, new friends and new life in western Canada. I buried our entire connection, all of the firsts we shared together and all of the feelings I had for him, somewhere deep. I wouldn't consider him a part of my story until I looked back over a decade later, after I graduated from university.

Whenever anyone asked me about my first kiss, I told them it was with my first girlfriend, Torie. Whenever a discussion about virginity came up, I told the story of how I had sex for the first time in a coworker's backyard with this hot girl I'd never met before and didn't see again afterward. I had effectively created a narrative of heterosexuality, focusing only on my romantic, emotional and sexual interactions with girls, while ignoring my history with boys.

Jett is no longer an unspoken truth to me. After coming out as trans queer in late 2013 and early 2014, I stopped leaving him out of my story whenever I told it. I also no longer hide other details of the way I experienced my queerness while growing up. Every crush I had on a boy, every time I tried on dresses and skirts, every time I watched gay porn, the years I secretly wore a sports bra under my shirts—it was all valid, and there was nothing wrong with any of it. I just wish I realized that much sooner.

FEAR AND SELF-LOATHING IN ALBERTA

Before I came out in the early 2010s, I experienced 15 years of hard self-denial, a mountain of anger toward both the world and myself, an aversion to intimate relationships and an intense fear of being perceived as gay. I participated in extremely unsafe sex practices that put me and those I was hooking up with at serious risk. At the core of it all was fear, driven by deep-seated guilt and shame around who I was and what I desired most. And all of those struggles drove my decisions in very harmful ways.

While I was in high school, I was so ashamed of my desires and attractions, so afraid anyone would think I wasn't straight, that I snuck out of my bedroom window late at night to meet queer men from the internet for hookups. While these midnight excursions were limited to oral sex, I didn't use any protection, I didn't know any of the adult men I met up with, and nobody knew where I was or whose car I was in.

Looking back, I feel like I barely dodged tragedy, and I'm lucky that nothing bad happened to me. Yet at the time, as queer representation in the media continued to be degrading and gayness was widely lambasted by my classmates at school, it felt like this was the only way for me to experience or explore sexual pleasure. And even then, I considered it nothing more than "getting off." I wasn't thinking about my identity, my sexuality, or more complex emotional needs, wants or desires. All of that was too scary to contemplate, and I did a lot of mental gymnastics to convince myself that no, I wasn't queer, it was just sex and all that mattered was that I was having it.

It was the same sad story for my gender identity and expression. Throughout my formative years, and well into my twenties, any time I felt compelled to explore my gender, the same pattern played out. I would try on "girl" clothes and makeup, I'd have a few amazing moments of feeling pretty and happy, and then I'd come down with overwhelming feelings of shame and guilt. I'd then ditch whatever clothes or supplies I had spent time collecting for myself, have a panic attack about it, and become angry with myself. I'd chastise myself and finally swear to never do it again. Those periods of repression would last months, sometimes even years. Until my late twenties, I leaned heavily into wearing baggy clothes, hiding my body from myself as much as others. I specifically avoided being topless, even in deeply intimate moments, until years after graduating university.

I went through a difficult period of my life from about the ages of 18 through 23. I was chain-smoking a pack and a half of cigarettes a day, drinking excessively—often to the point of becoming sick and blacking out—overeating, not looking after myself or my apartment, and struggling with heavy depression and thoughts of serious self-harm.

I also harboured a bitter misogynistic streak. Since I wasn't having sex at that point, and I was working so hard to repress my queer sexuality and gender identity, I felt angry at the world and all the women I knew for not seeing how great and how much of a "nice guy" I was. In typical toxic masculinity fashion, I attributed my lack of romantic and sexual fulfillment to women just having bad taste and choosing to be with guys I considered assholes. As far as I was concerned, I wasn't the problem; the problem was that others didn't realize how much better I'd be for them than their current boyfriend.

At my lowest point, it was so bad that I'm confident if I had been born any earlier, I'd have been navigating the lure of incels, **QAnon** and the cult of the **alt-right**. Luckily, I avoided all of that thanks to a mid-80s birthday and a chance at a fresh start. My glorious turnaround, and my queertastic rebirth, came not from some magical eureka moment, but rather through sports, of all damn things. While growing up, most of my experiences with sports were anxiety-inducing. The boys' teams I played on, both in school and outside of it, were laced with toxic masculinity, competitiveness and homophobic rhetoric. I ended up avoiding all sports as much as possible the instant that gym class was no longer a requirement, when I started university. While working as a freelance journalist in Moose Jaw in 2011, I was sent out to cover a skater recruitment night for the local roller derby league and immediately fell in love with the skaters, league and overall culture of the sport, in which players take on cheeky names and identities. A fast-paced, full-contact game played while wearing traditional four-wheeled roller skates, known as quad skates, roller derby has always been dominated by women and enbies, and has also always welcomed a tremendous number of queer and nonconforming officials and volunteers. The sport gives people from all walks of life a space to grow in more ways than you could imagine, which was a huge draw for me and quickly led to some pretty big revelations.

I began by slapping on a pair of quad skates to shakily try roller derby for myself. This test run led to a five-year journey of self-acceptance and personal growth unlike anything I had ever experienced. I mean, there's nothing quite as inspiring as badass queer babes in fishnets skating fast, hitting hard and riling up crowds of hundreds. In a matter of months, I went from seeing the world through the lens of the cisgender, heterosexual masculinity I was raised and socialized with to an eye-opening, mind-blowing exposure to queer and feminist magnificence.

It was revolutionary to me.

Roller derby quickly became a passion and special interest to me. After finishing my skater training with Moose Jaw Roller Derby, I was named the league's head referee and travelled with the team to officiate their away games around Saskatchewan and Manitoba. By 2014 I was so well established, with over 100 games under my belt as both a referee and a non-skating official (such as a scorekeeper, penalty tracker and jam timer), that I was frequently sought after for large tournaments across western and central Canada. As I found myself hanging around the likes of C-3PHO, Bazinga, Desi Deathwish and Lotta Shove, among others, in Regina's Pile O' Bones Derby Club, deep self-realizations came pretty quickly. The league members let me chill with them at the afterparties, made me feel welcome and accepted in the overall community, and eventually even invited me along to Pride events and fun nights at the gay clubs.

After such a long, dark period of self-loathing, I was finally starting to feel good about myself, to feel social, like I was part of something, and like I was worthy of having happy connections in my life. In November 2013, I came out as queer on a relatively successful roller derby blog I was running. Four months later, in March 2014, I came out again, this time as genderqueer.

Sadly, the sport wasn't quite as progressive about trans and nonbinary folks at that time, at least not in Saskatchewan and the other Prairie provinces. I could feel the shift in how people started to interact with me; I noticed a lot of discomfort and at times even animosity and fear about my presence at events. Many of the communities I used to feel safe visiting to referee didn't feel as welcoming and neighbourly anymore. Once that sense of safety and inclusion was gone, I lost all my passion for the sport and in the summer of 2015, I officially announced my retirement.

Yet despite the less-than-positive end of my time in roller derby, I still look back on the sport and my experiences with it rather fondly. While the sport may not have been ready to accept me for who I was at the time, it did a lot for me. Roller derby helped me realize I was ready to finally start accepting and embracing myself.

Fast-forward and now I'm a nearly forty-year-old queer, nonbinary, **polyamorous** author, editor and multiple-award-winning sex blogger. I've lived a tremendous amount in the decade since I've been out. I've had incredibly exciting queer relationships with fascinating people, hosted orgies at a riverside mansion with over 20 folks in attendance, fought hard for trans and queer rights across central Canada, and created a career for myself in the world of sexuality. I also know what I want out of my life and my interactions with others, and I'm thriving in romantically and sexually fulfilling relationships with my partners and play friends.

If I can alter my path from being a closeted, resentful, self-hatred-fueled misogynist to becoming a polyamorous **enboy** queer whose purpose in life is being happily gay and helping others embrace their gayness, then you too can make it through whatever is holding you back, friend! And you don't even need to get involved in a fringe sport to do it!

PRACTICING SELF-COMPASSION

My counsellor, Iris Akbar, has been working to support the LGBTQ+ community of Saskatoon, Saskatchewan, for many years now. One of the best things they ever told me was that I didn't have to love or forgive myself if I wasn't ready to, but I should show myself compassion as much as I possibly could. It's a lot of work. It takes tremendous effort, as you're often working against all those internalized shames, fears, self-doubts, insecurities and negative thoughts we went over earlier. Unsurprisingly, on some days, even just being somewhat nice to yourself might feel impossible, but that's OK! The trick here is to cut yourself a little slack about it and let yourself feel what you need to feel with little to no self-judgment or criticism.

It looks different for everyone, but practicing self-compassion is quite possibly the most accessible and effective method I've found to bring down my anxiety and slow down my doom spirals and intrusive thoughts. Whether it's my **rejection sensitivity dysphoria** (RSD) flaring up, a triggered trauma response or just regular ol' depression and anxiety, having patience and empathy for myself ultimately makes all the difference. By its very nature, self-compassion asks you to observe and be patient with yourself in moments of intense emotion, rather than putting pressure on yourself in pursuit of vigorous self-improvement. Instead of trying to "fix" something, to "solve" the feelings you're having, self-compassion is about being a conscientious observer of your emotional journey and thought patterns and learning to counter your habits of negative thinking with kindness and gentle declarations of validation.

Of course, self-compassion doesn't come naturally to most of us, especially neurodivergent folks and those with trauma. And it's especially hard if we were guilted and shamed for those identities while growing up.

As somebody with severe ADHD, anxiety and depression that impact my day-to-day life in a plethora of ways, it's easy to get frustrated at myself about my lack of focus, poor memory, executive-function troubles and exhaustion. Some days it takes me an hour or more to get out of bed and when I do, I'm faced with overwhelming forgetfulness, sensory-overload struggles, and that feeling that everything is going wrong and it's all my fault. If I'm not careful, self-critical thoughts can quickly take over, upset me and lead to a complete breakdown. My mind races, I ruminate on everything I'm doing wrong, I catastrophize about the impact that my perceived mistakes are having, and I engage in mean-spirited and self-deprecating criticism about whatever inadequacies my mind has decided to focus on.

That's the inner critic taking the lead.

The inner critic is an invalidating, fearmongering and demeaning voice that thrives on anxiety and self-loathing. The inner critic forms those judgmental thought patterns in our minds that further shame us about all the things we say, do and feel, at any given time. It contributes to you staying up late replaying the awkward social interactions you had that day. It leads you to continuously relive an embarrassing moment long after it happened. It's that negative self-perception that contributes to your decision to not dress the way you want, not pursue the relationships you desire, or not prioritize your sexual pleasure and fulfillment. The inner critic holds us in a self-degrading limbo.

In my case, the inner critic manifests as overwhelming and discouraging negative self-talk, which often parrots a lot of the fatphobic and queerphobic messaging I get from the rest of society, especially online. Most of the time I worry that I'm not "trans enough," that I don't come off as actually being queer, that I'm too old and too fat and too hairy to be attractive to anyone, and that it's only a matter of time before my partners realize they can do much better than me and move on. It's a weird form of self-critical thinking that also seems to include a great deal of gaslighting myself about my own experiences, traumas and perceptions.

Now, I can follow all of that negativity as it leads me into a hole, or I can take a deep breath and show myself empathy. While having a bad ADHD and executive-function day, "I'm gonna be late for my date and my partner is going to be angry at me" can become "it's OK to be late, I'm doing my best, and my partner will understand." As the inner critic inevitably spouts more harsh criticism, I can do my best to be ready with that sweet, sweet self-compassion! "Why am I such a goddamn mess" can become "it's OK to move at my own pace" and "nothing bad is going to happen if I slow down and take my time."

To counter your inner critic, ask yourself: How would you treat a good friend or a partner who was struggling with these same feelings? How would you respond to their negative self-talk? What advice would you give? How would you help support them, calm them and encourage them? The idea of self-compassion, then, is to support yourself in that same way.

Feeling insecure or unattractive? Try reminding yourself that it's OK to feel vulnerable, and that bodies are bodies, everyone's weight fluctuates, skin gets blemishes and ages, and none of that makes you—or anyone else—undesirable or unworthy of pleasure and fulfillment. Having trouble getting an erection, or having an orgasm, or receiving penetration? That's cool, no worries. It's OK for sex not to end with ejaculation or orgasm. It's OK to pleasure your partner or lover in other ways that aren't focused on penetration. It's OK to be anxious, distracted or otherwise unfocused during sex. You can still enjoy it in whatever way feels best for you, with the limitations you're experiencing!

And hey, you're not gonna be perfect at self-compassion. There are going to be tons of times when you'll forget to do it, or just won't have the energy to counter negative self-talk at all. That's OK! Self-compassion isn't about "fixing" anything. This practice isn't going to suddenly make bad thoughts and negative self-image vanish. But it is going to help you realize that you're capable of seeing yourself in a different, more positive way, and that can be enough to help you cope when the inner critic gets mean.

The more you show yourself compassion in all that you do, the more you'll be able to find what makes you feel sexy, desirable, confident, comfortable and happy. I'd even go as far as saying that practicing self-compassion has the potential to help you discover more about your sexual, emotional and romantic needs, wants, boundaries and desires than you ever thought possible. Just don't treat it like a miracle cure of some kind, because that's not what it is.

It's just a way for you to be a better friend to yourself when you really need one.

SHAKING OFF UNHELPFUL ADVICE AND TOXIC POSITIVITY

When people talk about breaking out of hurtful patterns and attracting the attention, relationships and experiences they want, they often talk about learning to love themselves.

Loving yourself, I've always been told, is the one and only way to become happy and confident; and by extension, it's also the only path toward finding love and companionship. I can't even begin to tell you how many times people told me that I wouldn't find love, pleasure or happiness until I started to love myself.

But I think it's OK not to love yourself right now if that's too daunting or difficult. And if you never end up fully loving yourself, that's OK too! If you end up just sort of liking yourself, or managing to tolerate your own company, that's fine. In fact, that's more than enough, and you deserve to celebrate that progress too. You're worthy of pleasure and affection and intimacy even if you're struggling with accepting yourself. Besides, most healing comes from community. Isolating yourself from it, and from potentially fulfilling relationships and other connections, until you reach some magical level of loving yourself is not only unrealistic, it's unfair—both to you and to the greater queer community, which needs you to be a part of it just as much as anyone else.

Instead of trying to force self-love, I suggest that what's truly important is being patient with, and observant of, yourself. It's striving to become an expert in all things "you," to understand how your experiences have shaped you, to be empathetic to your struggles, to forgive your mistakes, to allow yourself the space and freedom to grow and change, and to do all this work while avoiding the pitfall of becoming your own worst bully and abuser.

It's that self-compassion piece again, basically, with a healthy dose of self-reflection and consideration.

I've seen a lot of other vaguely shitty mantras out there too that just...don't help. Things like "have no fucks to give," "just stop caring what anyone else thinks," "nothing is ever as bad as it seems," "always look for the silver lining," "positive vibes only," and so on and so forth. As far as I'm concerned, all of these mantras suck. They're hollow, and they work by encouraging you to shame yourself about your negative thoughts and feelings, or even ignore them. In some cases, these sayings are outright invalidating. While positive thinking can help, it should never come at the expense of minimizing or negating your experiences. Even the bad ones. Because here's the thing: it's OK to feel bad. While the feelings may be hard right now, or even for a while, they are valid and it's important to acknowledge them and work toward understanding them as best you can.

Similarly, stuff like "do or do not, there is no try," "never give up," "you need to choose your happiness," "learn to let go," "don't dwell on it" and so on also rubs me the wrong way. In most cases, these sayings seem to operate on the premise that your problems are all in your mind, that they're not a big deal and shouldn't be a big deal to you either, and that getting through them should be super easy for you. So often, positive talk centres self-care as some choice that you can and must make, and posits that any resistance to that choice is a sign of your failures to overcome. If you can't "just do it," then clearly you're lazy, you're not working hard enough or you don't want it enough.

But I reject all of that wholeheartedly. There *is* try, you can absolutely give up on pursuits that are harmful and exhausting to you, it's OK to not be happy all of the time, it's OK to struggle and have negative thoughts, and you can take your journey at your own pace and with empathy for the experiences and struggles that make moving forward harder for you.

FINDING WHAT'S BEHIND YOUR ANXIETY AND STARTING SMALL

Self-compassion isn't some simple practice that you can just switch on (at least, it isn't for me!). It's tough when you just have so damn much anxiety, frustration, maybe even anger swirling about within you while you're trying to figure out who you are, or what you want, or how you could possibly even begin to feel desirable. As trans queer people, we don't have a lot of resources out there to guide us, regardless of what point we're at in our transition or journey.

If you're at the beginning of figuring out the culprit behind these big hang-ups, then the first step is asking yourself a pile of questions to determine what exactly is keeping you feeling stuck, or like you're unable to take any steps forward toward meeting your ideal sexual self. These questions can be particularly difficult to ask, but it's better to be real, direct and honest with yourself. Are you worried about how you might change? Are you concerned about what others might think? Are you anxious about how your family, friends, partners or lovers might react? Are you afraid of rejection, or of becoming undesirable somehow? How does the thought of possibly being in a queer relationship make you feel? Does wanting to feel sexy and desirable make you feel guilty or otherwise uncomfortable? Are you afraid of being trans queer? Is that fear an internal, personal one, or is it based on the negative messaging you see about LGBTQ+ folks?

If more questions come up while you're asking yourself these ones, that's a good thing! Let it all flow and lay itself out for you. You might be surprised to discover that in many cases, some degree of internalization is likely going on behind the anxieties you're experiencing. And while the bigger problems and snags may not be "solvable," they're all manageable with the right supports and tools at your disposal.

WHEN YOU'RE AFRAID OF WHAT MAY COME

Oftentimes fear is your body and mind's way of analyzing your safety, leading you to form your needs and boundaries, or possibly even indicating that your life is in need of some form of change. While it's good to experience emotions that raise important flags, if we don't listen to them and do the internal work they require, we can instead let them keep us from truly living our lives.

Fear doesn't happen spontaneously or entirely on its own. Something is always behind it—more often than not, it's a reaction to some perceived threat. In fact, if you thoroughly reflect on it, I'm confident that you'll realize your fear is based on some past experience or observed consequence that you want to avoid.

Maybe you've read a lot about people being disowned for being trans, nonbinary and/or queer and you don't want that to happen to you. Maybe you've heard of folks losing whole friend groups and struggling with isolation, and fear of that possibility is causing a lot of hesitancy. Maybe your church has talked a lot about LGBTQ+ folks suffering for eternity in the afterlife. Or maybe you've witnessed transphobic street harassment, heard the resentment and disgust in a loved one's voice while they discuss queer folks, or felt pressured to express animosity toward LGBTQ+ individuals.

These are real things that do, unfortunately, happen. I know, because they all happened to me. My family disowned me after I came out and I haven't heard from most of them in many years, with the exception of my mom, the one person who stood by me. However, I do want to remind you that every loss comes with the possibility of beautiful, enriching gains. I may have been abandoned by most of my family, but I've discovered many loving, caring and amazing trans and nonbinary queers who have been more supportive and encouraging than my blood relatives ever were.

So, even when you fear the worst, I want you to know that it's never actually the end of the world. While it's not always easy to see, and the world seems reluctant to focus on the abundance of trans, nonbinary and queer joy out there, happiness and fulfillment do exist for us. Don't let fear keep you from finding that for yourself.

INTERNALIZED QUEERPHOBIA AND TRANSPHOBIA

In addition to fear, observing and experiencing trans-phobia and queerphobia can lead us toward shame, guilt and self-doubt. The more negative discourse that surrounds you, the more difficult it's going to be to accept yourself, let alone others. Let's ask ourselves a few more questions to determine whether or not we may be directing anti-LGBTQ+ socialization inward, toward ourselves.

Do you feel uncomfortable around other trans and queer folks who proudly and confidently express themselves? Do public displays of affection from LGBTQ+ folks make you anxious or uneasy? Do you feel like your emotional, sexual or romantic needs and wants are somehow unnatural, wrong or sinful? If you experience attraction toward trans and nonbinary queers, do you wish that you didn't? Alternatively, do you feel angry when you see visibly trans and nonbinary queers in public because you wish that you could change your presentation to align more with your identity?

If you answered yes to any of these questions, that can be a big sign of some pretty entrenched internalization. Shame is often a huge culprit and can also materialize as feelings of disgust, anger or embarrassment that flare up whenever you make efforts to explore your sexuality and gender identity, or even think about doing so. And that can be scary. You might also experience a lot of resentment, jealousy or bitterness toward LGBTQ+ people who are out, thriving and having the relationships you long for but don't currently have. Gone unchecked, those resentments can also become judgmental, and may lead you into being outright transphobic or queerphobic. It's harmful to LGBTQ+ individuals if you project these feelings outward and will make finding your sexy, and finding yourself, all the more challenging.

So, what do you do about it? What work can you do to unpack this stuff? Honestly, I think a big part of it comes down to identifying where these beliefs originated and whether or not you still have any consistent sources of anti-LGBTQ+ sentiment impacting your perceptions. You've probably guessed how we're gonna do that by now...yep, more questions!

Were you raised in a deeply religious home that othered and vilified all things trans and queer? Do you harbour queerphobic or transphobic beliefs or sentiments? Does your friend group or social group put trans queer folks at the centre of a lot of denigrating jokes or discussions? Do you regularly read a lot of news or online media that is anti-LGBTQ+? All of these factors can have a profound effect on how you perceive yourself, both physically and emotionally.

It's worth the effort of doing all this self-reflection, and I believe that you're completely capable of working through those challenges to a place of comfort and self-acceptance. But that place is not going to come on its own. You have to get yourself there.

You can even start right now in small ways. That might mean minimizing the amount of time you spend with people who are actively bigoted toward LGBTQ+ folks, or blocking conservative media sources from your social media so that you're exposed to less queerphobic rhetoric. It could mean taking steps to change your social group a little, should those folks be making a lot of jokes and comments that contribute to your fear and shame. If you want to explore gender expression, getting yourself a little something and taking a tiny step forward can be immensely empowering. Maybe it's buying yourself some lipstick, maybe it's wearing panties or a sports bra under your clothes at home for the weekend, or maybe it's investing in a nice binder for your chest or picking up more gender-neutral clothing.

Or maybe it's just reading this book right now! That's progress. That's you doing something pretty big for yourself, and you should take a moment to be proud of that! Even thinking about any of this, in any capacity, is a lot. So, kudos to you!

In addition to all of the introspection and reading that you're doing here, I hope you'll also be able to find some trans queer–affirming community, friendships and, ideally, a counsellor or therapist. Many of us believe we have to do everything on our own, and that we shouldn't burden anybody else with our struggles, feelings or mental health. The result is that many of us suffer in silence, alone, without any of the tools and supports that are vital to our healing and growth.

While it's true that you should be careful about putting unreasonable expectations or pressure on others, because it's nobody else's responsibility to unpack these things or "fix" how you're feeling, it's also OK to find like-minded people who you know will uplift and encourage you and with whom you can share some of your feelings and experiences in a mutually supportive way. It's OK to need help, and to seek it out.

Finding queer community can be an especially important piece of this process because part of that fear, shame and guilt also comes from some of the queerphobia and transphobia that you may have internalized. Don't be too hard on yourself; given how prevalent it is, a degree of internalization is hard to avoid. As I've already mentioned, I too had a great deal of trouble accepting myself because of my own negative and harmful opinions and understanding of trans queers, which came from my social upbringing.

Be prepared for the hard and awkward work of undoing this internalization, though. It never feels good to realize that you've been holding onto harmful and offensive notions about others, even if it's been mostly internal up until this point. Chances are high that you're eventually going to say something that will garner an angry or upset reaction from somebody else. Try to take a deep breath and understand where that anger and upset comes from. Many trans queer folks have to deal with invalidating, demeaning and insulting misinformation, judgment, abuse and more quite regularly. If you're able to empathize with those reactions, you'll likely find it a lot easier to take accountability for how you may have caused offense, and to understand where you may need to do some more self-education.

But maybe you can get a jump on some of that now by asking yourself about your stances on a few major LGBTQ+ issues! Do you think that queer people are maybe too sensitive about everything and should count their blessings? Are you worried that the trans queer people you'll potentially date might have a higher chance of giving you sexually transmitted infections (STIs)? Do you think that "real" trans people all want to pass and "fully" transition within a system based on the **gender binary**, and that nonbinary and gender-nonconforming people aren't real or valid? Do you think that trans activists are going too far and are pressuring kids into making major medical decisions they may later regret?

If you answered yes to any of these questions, that's definitely a sign that some degree of queerphobic and transphobic messaging has stuck. All of these questions reflect right-wing talking points about trans queer people.

Right-wing actors across North America and many other regions around the world are pursuing legislation designed to silence, control and in many cases, eradicate basic human rights and protections for LGBTQ+ people. These beliefs are all steeped in a lot of myths and disinformation about human sexuality and gender.

Just remember, unlearning the harmful and dehumanizing things you may have been raised to believe about trans queer people doesn't just help others. It also helps you and will go a long way toward helping you achieve your goals of finding your sexy and feeling more empowered in your queer self. If you're looking for places to find better information about trans queer people and the issues they face, I highly recommend avoiding most mainstream news outlets and social media sites where misinformation rules. Instead, look toward trans-positive sources that better represent LGBTQ+ people and the major struggles we're currently facing. (Check out the resources section at the end of this book for suggestions.)

DEVELOPING YOUR SELF-CARE TOOLKIT

While I've been in the practice of unpacking all of my trauma, insecurity and fear through my deeply personal, intimate sex blog for the past decade, and now writing this book, you don't need to be so publicly vulnerable in order to sort through and unpack all your hard feelings. You can work on your self-acceptance, understand and experience your personal identity, and connect with your sensual, sexual self in many other ways. Maybe it's journaling, creating art, making music, hiking, engaging in faith-based practices, starting a new hobby, joining a club, running or otherwise finding an outlet for your processing efforts.

When it comes to facing the big feels on a daily basis, one practice that's always helped me is grounding and mindfulness. When I'm feeling incredibly overwhelmed, I like to remind myself that while many things are outside of my control, I can almost always take command of my breathing. It frequently helps me to take a moment to physically assess where I am through what I can see, hear and feel. I try my best to focus only on those measurable, disconnected sensations and observations, rather than putting too much thought into what's stressing me out. The idea isn't to solve anything; it's to defuse the emotions and anxieties I'm experiencing at that exact moment. I look at what I'm feeling, acknowledge it, and then turn my attention away from it completely to instead take in and let out several deep breaths. In those moments, I can bring myself into my environment more and calm my nerves by physically grounding myself in the present to reduce anxiety and shame spirals.

Meditation can offer a more intellectual, perspective-altering and perhaps even spiritual experience. You can meditate in numerous ways, including the simple grounding exercise I just described. However, meditation can also involve a more thoughtful approach to self-enlightenment and a concerted effort to change your way of thinking about, or experiencing, your life. These more intensive practices can also focus on your emotions or thoughts, or can be more abstract, like considering the space you're in, what it means, what it feels like, and what "space," in both the physical and conceptual senses, even is. But I'm not as well versed with this practice, and I know that if done without any consideration, some forms of meditation can lead to more anxiety. So be sure to do some research and maybe even reach out to a local expert to discuss what you're looking for and how you could begin.

I'm also a big fan of creating and sustaining your emotional reserve. Again, it looks different for everyone, but what you're basically doing is making a source you can return to for positive affirmations and empowerment. As I'm a very visual person, my emotional reserve comes in the form of folders on my computer that I can open and look through. In these folders, I keep images, documents, news stories and other files that lift my spirits, make me happy and make me proud of myself. These folders are filled with pictures of me and my partners smiling, cuddling and having a great time together. Seeing them reminds me that I am loved, wanted and valued by people. I also have screenshots of positive reviews for my books, blog comments from readers who were inspired or helped by my site, nice messages I've received from partners and friends, evidence of some of my cooler accomplishments and experiences—basically things that help me build an uplifting personal narrative.

If a folder on your computer doesn't sound like your thing, you can also print off documents or photos and put them in a journal or photo album, or on your fridge or a bulletin board somewhere in your home. Wherever this emotional reserve needs to exist for you to use it most efficiently and comfortably is where you need to put it!

Further, I highly recommend taking the time to read about other people's journeys. To help you reconnect with, explore, embrace or rediscover your intimate self, you can peruse a wide variety of books, blogs and other work from content creators who share their own experiences for the benefit of others.

Reading work by other trans queers definitely helps—especially considering how much hard and emotionally draining work goes into unpacking and reprogramming all that **cisnormativity**, **heteronormativity**, fatphobia, ableism, racism, ageism and more that trickles down through societal messaging and cultural ideals around our identities and bodies.

SIGNS YOU MAY NEED SOME EXTRA HELP

Sometimes our fears, shame and guilt come from negative and hurtful personal experiences, not only from societal messaging. These experiences may include childhood trauma, intimate partner violence, physical or sexual assault, severe breaches of trust or safety, neglect, bullying, dangerous or uncomfortable living environments, demeaning criticism and other forms of abuse. All of these experiences add to the challenges of unpacking your feelings, especially the more invasive and negative ones, particularly if they have been reinforced over and over again through past interactions that may have been designed to control or manipulate you into behaving or thinking according to an abuser's wishes.

If you've had these kinds of experiences, or other harmful ones, keep an eye out for signs that may indicate you could use a little extra help with everything you've been experiencing. For me, a big sign can be addictions. During my darkest periods of depression, anxiety and internal strife, I found it a lot easier to retreat into a bottle of alcohol than to address the negative thoughts and overwhelming emotions that I was having. Struggling with substances doesn't make you a bad person by any means, but it can be quite harmful to your mental health and physical wellness if it gets out of hand. Waking up hungover often, turning to hard drugs, struggling with your feelings about eating and food, or leaning into increasingly frequent unsafe or impulsive sexual encounters—these behaviours may indicate a developing addiction problem. In these cases, I feel that it's pretty imperative to consider including a mental health professional in your healing journey.

Other signs that you could benefit from professional support can be a little harder to pinpoint until they start affecting your relationships and day-to-day life. Maybe you've been getting less and less rest, having more frequent anxiety attacks, struggling with remembering to eat, or experiencing dissociation or increased memory issues. Or maybe you're lashing out a lot, having intense arguments with everyone, feeling backed into a corner, and finding yourself overwhelmed with anger and defensiveness. Perhaps what started off as a few cancelled plans has become pretty intense self-isolation, or maybe recent experiences have you so afraid of going outside that just existing is becoming a problem. Could be that you've been feeling so down about yourself that you're barely looking at yourself in the mirror while you brush your teeth, and that's morphed into some pretty intense resentment of others who look the way you wish you did. These scenarios can all be big indicators that professional aid is needed, though I'll be the first to admit how difficult it is to know that you're having a particularly hard time until the impact of it fully hits you. You might even need somebody to gently point out to you that they've noticed changes in your behaviour. It can be hard to hear these comments from family members, friends or partners, but try your best not to lash out and instead listen to why people who care about you are concerned. In all likelihood, their concern comes from a place of genuine care. It might not be until your friend mentions that you've cancelled plans with them for the fifth consecutive time that you realize you've been isolating for months.

Be it a counsellor, psychiatrist or therapist, somebody with the formal training and education to help guide and empower you can be paramount to navigating these situations, especially if they happen to be well versed in LGBTQ+ terminology, issues and experiences. Sadly, that's not always so easy to find, but if you happen to have a local Pride organization, or some form of trans or LGBTQ+ or queer support group or organization, I strongly recommend reaching out to inquire about trans queer mental health supports. Many organizations and groups have regularly updated lists of safe and inclusive professionals and practices. Some cities even have dedicated LGBTQ+ counselling services on site, or in partnership with local hospitals, clinics or private practices.

Do a little research to find somebody who can support you with the challenges you're facing, and who you're not going to have to educate over the course of your first several sessions. Find yourself somebody who already gets it, and who is vetted by your community as a safe, affirming and empowering support.

Never forget, it's OK to be in a bad way. So many things make it hard to exist in this world as a trans or nonbinary queer person. And it's OK to need help, and to ask for it. There's no shame in using the support resources you have at hand, both the ones within your community and those you've worked hard to develop yourself.

CHAPTER 4
MAKING YOUR PERSONAL MANTRAS

Now that we've gone through the myriad ways that transphobia and queerphobia have been pounded into our collective perspective, let's take a crack at creating some new internal messaging to counteract all of that negative noise. Because here's the kicker: most of the reasons trans queer folk tend to not feel sexy, desirable, lovable or wanted stem from a combination of how cisgender, thin, white bodies are shown as being the norm across society and how we've been taught to perceive ourselves in relation to that norm. If we don't address this stuff, we end up burying it and letting it continue to fester and inform our opinions of ourselves and our partners and lovers, which can become extremely harmful in the long term. And we can't have that, because that's how you stay stuck and deprive yourself of truly empowering, affirming and fulfilling bonds!

For trans and nonbinary queer individuals, the effects of transphobic and queerphobic messaging can include self-doubt, a fear of intimacy, social anxiety, insecurities, low self-worth, body dysmorphia, gender dysphoria and many other overwhelming internal struggles. The messaging creates this narrative, on both a social and personal level, that only people with specific types of bodies and identities are ever going to feel happy and fulfilled in their relationships, and that pleasure is only available to those who meet the acceptable societal standards for it.

A helpful place to start all of this hard internal work for yourself is to make an empowering framework of mantras and uplifting messaging to build from. Your mantras are your own personal slogans to hype you up and cheer you on in your pursuits. They are statements you can come back to again and again and again, daily if needed. You can say them out loud, read them if you want to, and use them as reminders that you're on the right track. If employed strategically, your mantras can be the first building blocks as you work to bolster your self-worth.

Keep your mantras short and easy to remember, and think about how they directly relate to yourself. Treat them as uplifting assertions and points of guidance that centre you and help you to better prioritize your pleasure, happiness and boundaries.

DEFINING YOUR CORE VALUES

A big part of creating mantras for yourself is thinking about your personal core values and how they have the potential to impact everything from your self-perception to the boundaries you need in your life. Your values define an awful lot of your views, both internally and externally, or in other words, both personally—how you see yourself—and interpersonally—how you see others. Applying your core values to your mantras can give them a bigger kick and make them feel a lot more meaningful to you.

Some of my main core values are communication, compassion, creativity and authenticity. These are the essential building blocks to my life, my identity and all of the bonds and relationships I forge.

Communication is my highest priority. After years of living in abusive and controlling homes, with both toxic partners and family, I need to feel that I can express myself safely and truthfully, without fear of anger, aggression or substantial conflict. If I do not feel safe communicating my needs, wants, desires, experiences and boundaries, or communicating my identity, then I do not feel safe at all.

Compassion for myself, my partners and my community is also of paramount importance to me. I strive to be sympathetic not only to the feelings, experiences and needs of others, but to my own. And I feel that striving comes through in the mantras I tend to use for personal growth and healing.

Creativity also continues to be something that I cherish. As a lifelong writer and storyteller, creativity has been crucial to my mental health, wellness and self-understanding. Freedom of speech, expression and art—expressed with passion, empathy and the desire to inspire, uplift and empower both others and oneself—are absolute musts to me.

Finally, authenticity in everything rounds out my values in a big way. As an out, loud and proud autistic, polyamorous trans queer with ADHD, authenticity is pretty crucial to who I am, and who I strive to be. Aside from needing to feel like I can safely be myself, I am most drawn to, and find most attractive and comfortable, people who live true to themselves and are proud of who they are. Authenticity also applies to pursuing my passion, living where I feel happiest, doing what brings me the most joy and speaking my truth in all that I do.

How about your core values? Remember that your personal values can encompass a broad range of qualities, including community, stability, personal development, spirituality, independence, privacy, dependability, wisdom, kindness and so much more. Once you get some of your values in place, you'll find making your own mantras a much less daunting task!

For example, if one of your core values is community, that's going to have a big impact on the framing around your mantras. While some may be focused on you as an individual, such as "I will find my people," others might be more socially based, along the lines of "I deserve to feel safe in my community" or "I am worthy of acceptance and respect from my family and friends." In contrast, perhaps a huge core value of yours is individuality. If that were the case, your mantras would reflect more focus on, and affirmations of, the self. Some more individualistic mantras may include "it's OK for me not to want a traditional relationship," or "I'm allowed to take space for myself," or even "my boundaries and privacy are important and deserve respect."

To aid you in starting to create your own, I offer the following six of my personal favourite mantras. These examples are meant to help you keep focused on yourself and to absolve yourself of internalizing any of the unfair pressures that come with working on your personal growth and your intimacy needs.

AFFIRMING MANTRA 1:
"I'VE BEEN DOING MY BEST" OR "IT'S OK FOR ME TO STRUGGLE WITH ALL OF THIS."

Wherever you are in your journey, at this exact moment, is valid. Maybe you're feeling overwhelmed while just starting to come out as trans queer, maybe you've been out for years but are realizing new facets to your identity and how they affect your self-perception, or maybe you're struggling with your self-worth after getting out of a major relationship. Whatever the case may be, I'm willing to bet that if you stop to think about it, you'll realize you've had a lot going on. Never forget that you're doing your best with what you've got.

In just the past decade alone, I've come out as trans queer; been disowned by my father and sister; got married and then divorced; and struggled through employment discrimination, street harassment, abusive living situations, unstable housing, debt collection, physical violence and all the associated PTSD that goes along with all of the above. That's lots to deal with, and then add in the fact that I'm autistic and have ADHD, anxiety and depression. Not to mention that we've all been surviving a devastating and traumatizing pandemic that's still ongoing as we near the mid-2020s. So, yeah, I've had to give myself some slack for not having it all figured out yet!

Same goes for you. It's valid to feel frustrated about not having a better grasp of yourself and your needs, wants and desires, but you still have plenty of time and so many exciting things to look forward to. Don't get too wrapped up in hating and blaming yourself for not feeling great about who you are, how you look, or what has or hasn't happened for you yet. You've done your best so far, and now it's time to learn, grow and explore further!

AFFIRMING MANTRA 2:
"IT'S OK TO PRIORITIZE MYSELF."

Yes, really! I've always disliked how much society tends to frame centring oneself as being selfish, as if being selfish is inherently a bad thing, which it most definitely is not. Sure, being selfish to the harm and detriment of those around you isn't cool. However, prioritizing your own needs and wants without considering or worrying about everyone else all of the time can be a powerful step in breaking free from negative self-talk, fear, shame and all that other internalized junk.

Letting your own happiness, self-worth, fulfillment and pleasure take the lead more often in your life is just as important as putting other people's needs first—and it might even be more important. Make a habit of asking yourself what you need to feel safe, comfortable and happy. And remind yourself that it's completely fair to take whatever steps you need in order to get yourself there.

AFFIRMING MANTRA 3:
"I HAVE COMPLETE AND UTTER
AUTONOMY OVER MYSELF."

Whether you're coming to terms with your gender iden-tity or sexual orientation, or you've already done that work and are now searching for ways to bolster your confidence, or you want to rethink and redefine your sexual self, it all comes down to you. Only you can decide what and how much you want to do. Any advice or guidance from anyone, be it me or somebody else, is exactly that: advice—suggestions for paths that you could take, and how you could take them. In the end though, what you do, and how much of it you do, is your call.

Maybe you just want a super-queer haircut (I always suggest the staple sidecut), maybe you want to dye your hair, or maybe you want to update your entire wardrobe to better reflect who you are. Could be that you've been experiencing attraction to genders similar to your own, or way outside of the binary, and you want to diversify your dating experiences. Maybe you just want to start exploring your own gender in a more sexually intimate environment, or find affirming ways to dress when you go out that make you feel desirable and amazing.

Perhaps you've done a lot of the more exploratory aspects of figuring out your identity, and you're starting to consider various medical transition steps, such as laser hair removal, hormone replacement therapy, top surgeries such as a **mastectomy**, **mammoplasty**, or breast augmentation, or bottom surgeries such as an **orchiectomy**, **hysterectomy**, **vasectomy**, or **vaginoplasty**.

Whatever the case may be, whatever you need to do to feel happy and comfortable with your trans queer self, your needs are valid. Don't let anyone guilt, shame or argue you out of doing what you need to do for yourself. Your body, your rules.

You have so many options out there to consider when it comes to steps you can take toward feeling better in your body, your identity, your relationships and yourself. And there's no one right or wrong way to do it. Your way, whatever it may be, is right—so long as it's right by you.

AFFIRMING MANTRA 4:
"I AM NOT RESPONSIBLE FOR
THE FEELINGS OF OTHERS."

One of the hardest parts of exploring your sexuality, gender and other deeply intimate aspects of yourself is the pressure and judgment that tends to come from those around us. Family members, friends, partners and even peers in our community sometimes take personally the choices we make for ourselves. As I mentioned in the last chapter, when I first came out as trans, I was immediately bombarded with an endless stream of opinions from everyone around me. Social acquaintances offered me unsolicited advice on how to "look more femme"; LGBTQ+ peers had an awful lot to say about the pronouns and terminology I used to describe my experiences; my dad and sister were deeply embarrassed about how open I was about my transition and queerness. I felt tremendous pressure to consider how everyone else was feeling about this deeply personal journey I was undertaking. It took a lot away from it for me, and made everything so much harder.

If you're feeling similarly overwhelmed with anxiety about not upsetting everyone, if it's starting to negatively affect how you feel about things, if it's influencing your decisions in ways that mean compromising what you actually need and want for yourself—please try your absolute best to remind yourself that none of it is your responsibility. Not a damn thing! Any anger, discomfort, frustration, shame or fear that others feel about you is their deal, not yours.

Stay your course! Stay true to who you are and what you need.

AFFIRMING MANTRA 5:
"IT'S OK TO CHANGE MY MIND."

A lot of people seem to think that if you haven't known you were trans queer your whole life, or if you can't "choose" between one identity or another, that must mean you're incapable of defining yourself in any reliable way. Nope! That's bullshit. It's just not that simple.

Change is OK. In your journey of self-discovery, in pursuit of your happiness, wellness and pleasure, the last thing you'll want to do is be resistant to it. If you've already come out as gay, but now feel like you're maybe actually bisexual or pansexual, cool! You can swap those labels! They're not fixed, and you don't have to be either. Or maybe you're well along your way into FTM or **MTF** transition, yet you've discovered that gender fluidity and nonconformity is your thing and you want to use they/them pronouns, and maybe change up your transition goals. Sweet! Do that!

We're all constantly learning, growing and evolving as people, and a big part of that evolution includes our identities and the terminology we use to describe our experiences. I mean, people change their labels and identifiers all the time, even outside of the context of sex and gender. Some people identify as boys, then men, and perhaps eventually husbands, dads and granddads should they choose to marry or have kids. Some identify as girls, then women, and maybe eventually wives, moms and grandmas. Identity isn't static. Hell, in my lifetime I've been a lot of things. I've been a son, a boy, a crossdresser, trans, trans femme, a trans woman, genderfluid and nonbinary—and now I'm feeling more in tune with being a genderqueer (sometimes nonbinary) trans boi. I also love the term **genderfaun**, referring to a form of genderfluidity based in queer masculinity under which people do not experience any connection to women-aligned identities or identifiers. It speaks to me pretty deeply. I'm just a trans queer boi! I've also been a student, a graduate, employed, unemployed, a roller derby referee, a freelance writer, a community service worker, a blogger, an author and an editor.

All of that is to say that it can take a long time to find the language to describe ourselves and our experiences. Along the way, we're bound to use what feels right at the time, but if further self-evaluation leads to new identities, desires, needs and wants, don't shut yourself off from those possibilities. Besides, the terms that best describe your experiences of your identity may not even exist yet!

AFFIRMING MANTRA 6:
"I'M ALLOWED TO GO AT MY OWN PACE."

I get it. When I was ready to put in all the good, hard work to find my sexy, I wanted to jump into it headfirst. And in a lot of ways, I did. I don't have any real regrets about that, even though rushing forward did lead to some hurt and discomfort at times. But that's not going to work for everyone. I think that moving at your own pace, whatever that may be, is best.

Giving yourself time to process what you're thinking, feeling and wanting goes a long way to ensure that you don't push yourself too hard or find yourself in uncomfortable situations, unable to clearly express your limits, before you've fully understood your needs, wants and boundaries.

And hey, if you decide to go hard at all of this, that's OK too! Just try to be safe and listen to what your body is telling you, friends!

Now it's time to make your own mantras. Start from scratch, or use some of the examples I've provided above as a jumping-off point to develop the mantras that you'll use going forward as you work to embrace yourself and find your sexy. They'll be especially helpful in the next chapter as we look at challenging and breaking free from the toxic social systems that frequently hinder personal growth for trans queers.

CHAPTER 5

SAYING NO TO TRADITIONAL GENDER ROLES AND OTHER TOXIC IDEALS

Transphobia and queerphobia are hard to navigate as a trans queer seeking self-empowerment. These forms of bigotry are ingrained within our culture, education systems, medical services, social communities (at least the cisgender, heterosexual ones) and politics, and they make life needlessly difficult for trans queers. When you have to exert so much effort to simply get through your day-to-day life, let alone face fears about anti-LGBTQ+ laws, policies and movements, it can take a lot out of you.

But there's much more to contend with, because at the core of the bigotries we experience lie a number of long-standing and toxic traditions, ideals and social systems. To start overcoming some of the prejudices we face, especially if we've internalized them, we need to look at what's underneath them and work to dismantle those underlying factors for ourselves in a way that minimizes the harm they can do to our lives.

In this chapter, I'm going to be talking quite critically about traditions and ideals such as passing as a person with a binary gender, finding a monogamous partnership and having children—some of which you may desire. There's nothing wrong with wanting to follow these paths yourself. However, it's important to address how society often presents these conventional paths as expectations and norms in such a way that creates tons of pressure and stifles any deviation from them. Spending some time thinking about these ideals in the bigger context of cisnormativity and heteronormativity can be quite enlightening and help you check in with yourself to ensure that you're not feeling guilty, ashamed or expected to be or do something that doesn't feel entirely right for you.

BINARY (CIS)GENDER ROLES AND EXPECTATIONS

Despite the fact that queerness and gender non-conformity have been documented in civilizations and communities throughout recorded history, we still see a wide lack of acceptance, support or consideration. Schools, churches, public spaces, governmental and social services, hospitals, clinics, sports teams, changing rooms, bathrooms, gyms and more are all built for cisgender people and formulated around the gender binary of boys and girls, men and women, males and females. Those who exist outside of that framework are often met with everything from judgmental staring to full-on harassment, threats and even physical violence.

These various forms of transphobia exist largely because of cisnormativity, which describes a social system based on the assumption that everyone identifies with the gender they were assigned at birth and all people are inherently cisgender. Since most of the world operates under cisnormativity, trans and nonbinary people often experience profound prejudice, discrimination, violence and general antagonism. Sadly, cisnormativity can also become internalized in such a way that trans people deny themselves the opportunity to transition or force themselves to transition in a way they think they "should."

Cisnormativity begins to impact our lives long before we're even fully conscious of our existence. While in the womb, some of us are slapped with a binary gender identity based on the binary sex defined by the appearance, or absence, of a penis on a display screen during a prenatal ultrasound. If your physician examines the ultrasound and can see a penis, your parent is informed that you are a boy, whereas if there is no penis, you may be categorized as a girl. The frustrating bit is that it's not even 100% accurate because ultrasounds are less clear than the crappy security-camera footage from a supermarket, and the doctor won't know whether or not their interpretation is accurate until you've been born and a more thorough examination is conducted. And yet, this designation of a baby's sex, even when it's not 100% certain, is often taken at face value and used to assign them a gender, which then informs how parents prepare for the arrival of their baby. Gender designation dictates every single facet of our lives. It determines how we're raised, what clothes we're dressed in, how we're socialized, what kinds of jobs and careers we'll be considered for, how much we'll be paid, and what our role will be in the formation of the nuclear family.

Going counter to gendered expectations in any way threatens the status quo. Therefore, in the eyes of those who benefit from gender-based structures and hold privilege within them, queerness and gender diversity must be squashed, denied, outlawed and denigrated.

That's why so much anti-LGBTQ+ messaging centres around one key factor: family. Every cruel, and prejudiced, and dehumanizing thing that hard conservatives say and do toward the gender- and sexually diverse community is to "protect" and "ensure the safety" of the "normal," everyday, Western nuclear family. By making trans queers the enemy of the family unit, by referring to us as "groomers" and suggesting that we are a danger to women and children, anti-LGBTQ+ forces perpetuate our dehumanization and try to remove our rights.

But that doesn't mean you have to force yourself to bow to any of it. To exist as your authentic trans queer self in the face of all of that garbage is, frankly, brave as heck. Maybe that means pursuing the queer partnerships you desire, maybe it means presenting yourself through your clothing and self-expression without shame, maybe it means staying single and nourishing platonic connections, or maybe it means seeking out multiple ethical, fulfilling polyamorous relationships. Truth is, there are many ways to experience romance, sex, pleasure and happiness in this life—so don't let cisnormativity rain on your parade, limit your joy or hold you back from your desires.

PASSING PRESSURE AND
THE IDEALIZED TRANS

Trans queers experience the harm of gender roles and expectations in some specific ways—not just in terms of how we're treated by cishet individuals, but also, sadly, in how we treat each other and ourselves. One of the most insidious of these harms that exist in queer culture, at least in my opinion, is the issue of "passing pressure." This term describes the toxic social expectation that transitioning is only OK if it is done discreetly and according to the gender binary, and that the only acceptable trans people are those whose end goal is to "fit in" and to appear as cishet as possible in their "new" sex and gender identity. While quite predominant in cishet spaces, passing pressure is also sadly perpetuated by some trans queers who, desperate for the acceptance of friends, family, loved ones and society, project these expectations onto others within the community. In some cases, this projection takes the form of guilt and shaming tactics, or even condemnation and anger.

While it is valid to identify and express yourself as a woman or a man, the gender binary should never be forced upon others. Those members of the trans community who truly believe in the gender binary to the point where they engage in toxic levels of gatekeeping, invalidation and transphobia cause great harm to individuals who already face tremendous adversity as they struggle to understand themselves as nonbinary or otherwise nonconforming. Some of these binary-focused trans folks may inhabit trans queer spaces, but they may do so with a degree of resentment, as they may not identify as trans, and may believe that any gender nonconformity, even a slight deviation from the "full transition" narrative, is a threat to their own validity. In their view, if you're not doing the "all-in" commitment of passing as a cis person like they strive to, including undergoing hormone replacement therapy and all the necessary surgeries, then you're not "really trans." It's a pervasive and deeply harmful narrative especially when used to guilt or shame others into thinking they're somehow not being themselves "right."

It's basically **gender essentialism** from a slightly different perspective. In this belief, transphobic folks insist that there are distinct, fixed and intrinsic qualities to men and women that make it impossible for trans men or trans women to ever be accepted in the same breath as cisgender people. The same transphobic belief system underlies the notions that you have to want to pass in order to be trans, that only trans men and trans women are valid, and that transition is only authentic when it is medical and surgical. These ideas frequently fall under the umbrella of **transmedicalism**, aka transmed or truscum: the belief that trans people who don't experience much dysphoria—or don't wholly reject everything about their body and seek thorough medical intervention immediately—don't qualify as trans.

What this ideology fails to realize is that even if trans people checked every single box of binary gender conformity, which have by and large been defined by cishet people as the guiding principles of what they'd maybe consider acceptable for trans people, transphobia would still exist and trans people would still struggle to be accepted in many spaces. Trans people throwing each other under the bus for not meeting some toxic ideal for transness isn't doing anybody any good at all. So I strongly recommend you avoid people with this transmedicalist worldview, as they tend to operate under the assumption that any and all gender nonconformity and genderqueerness threatens their own validity and therefore must be challenged, undermined and admonished.

Once upon a time, I was convinced that in order to feel happy, safe and fulfilled in my life after coming out as queer and trans, I had to strive to pass as a "woman." In addition, I also had to feel uncomfortable with, or outright hate, my body. I mean, if trans people don't hate their bodies, if they don't want to change every single thing about themselves in order to live and be perceived as the "other gender," then are they even trans?

Of course they fucking are!

But passing pressure is a beast to work through, especially early in your coming-out process, when you often turn to a community for guidance and support. I was so excited, taking the first major steps I'd ever taken in a public way, and rather than being welcomed with joyous celebration and support, I was mostly met with criticism and judgment. Well-meaning allies gave me unsolicited advice on how I could "look prettier" and "look more like a woman," and trans women assumed I was going to go for all of the medical transition things and insistently asked me when I'd start on hormone replacement therapy (**HRT**) and get bottom surgery. But nobody ever asked how I felt about myself. Instead, everyone around me kept making assumptions about what being trans meant for me, without considering my thoughts on the matter.

I can't even begin to tell you how many trans queer people told me that I wasn't trans if I liked having a penis, or didn't want to start on HRT. I heard numerous times that there were only two genders, even for trans people, and that being nonbinary or gender nonconforming was just a phase on the way to being "really trans." It sucked, and these comments became an inner monologue that filled me with shame, fear and insecurities during what should have been the most exciting self-exploration times of my entire life.

Yet no matter how hard I tried to look as femme and typically sexy as I could, I was never able to reach any of those cisnormative ideals in the slightest. I've always been a stocky person, with broad shoulders, a big chest, and thick arms and legs, all covered in rich and dark body hair. Rather than disliking my body due to dysphoria and a longing to be a woman, which was never a need of mine, I started to just outright hate myself entirely for being this unattractive being that would never find their identity and feel good in themself.

In reality, I was as genderqueer as they come. But sadly, that realization didn't come until well after a long period of social pressure and self-loathing.

Fact is, a socially idealized trans person exists, and that model is almost always white, slim, femme and unmistakably cis passing. She's also (tellingly) nice to cis people (despite any abuse she receives from them), she doesn't "make waves," she doesn't speak out in ways that make "allies" uncomfortable, she doesn't march in protests (just fun Pride parades), and she tends to put assimilation and conformity above the needs of her most marginalized peers—queer and trans people of colour (**QTPOC**), sex workers, newcomers, queer folks with disabilities and more. Meanwhile, trans men and genderqueer folks aren't even considered as part of these equations.

Essentially, the ideal trans person I was expected to become, the archetype I was introduced to early on, was as close as possible to a neurotypical cishet woman. At the very least, I'd need to be a well-behaved queer and try to do my best to "fit in."

Now, I'm not saying that wanting to fit in is bad. I'm not saying that you're a terrible trans queer person for striving to pass as a binary gender. But I am saying that presenting one narrative of transness as correct and universal is brutally dangerous and harmful to everyone to whom it doesn't apply. And believe it or not, far more people exist outside of that narrative than you might think.

I did eventually hit a breaking point. It took going back into the closet for a while, and even distancing myself from my local Pride community, but the day finally came when I stopped shaving and I embraced my fat, hairy, rude ass.

I was tired of escaping one set of expectations, only to be forced under a new set repackaged as "transition." I was tired of forcing myself into a narrative that wasn't for me, because that was the only narrative others said was acceptable. I was tired of the ingrown hairs, the razor burn and the stress that came from the pursuit of smoothness.

Most of all, I was tired of constantly chasing unattainable outcomes and standards that I set for myself, not because I wanted them, but because I thought I needed them to survive. I thought I needed HRT in order to pass so I could blend in, be safe, be respected and receive love. I thought I needed laser hair removal to look nice, to be attractive in a dress or skirt, to be accepted socially or to get a job.

And I got angry.

Too often, we're told that anger is a bad thing. We're told that it's destructive, antagonizing and off-putting. We're told that it's counterproductive, that it pushes our allies away, makes us unreasonable, encourages our abusers to continue abusing us, and subverts all of our advocacy and activism efforts.

That's bullshit, and it's victim blaming.

Anger is not an inherently bad emotion. No emotion is inherently bad or good. And like every other emotion, anger has an energy that can be harnessed either positively or negatively.

My anger has helped me stand up to harassers, abusers, bigots and more. It has helped me set boundaries for myself that have improved my mental, emotional and physical wellness. It has empowered me to embrace myself, to speak out, to share my experiences. It has led me to practice self-compassion and embrace what makes me feel best in myself. It has allowed me to reframe my masculinity, my hair, my beard and my body in queer-affirming ways.

Most of all, though, it has motivated me to create content, resources and supports for others that I couldn't find when I needed them.

I hope you find that power in your anger too.

ALL BODIES ARE DIFFERENT
(AND REALLY WEIRD)

Despite how often specific physical traits are idolized as being the "most attractive," there are no "perfect" bodies, and even those that may seem like they fall close to that supposed camp are riddled with imperfections. The pursuit of perfection, in a society that constantly moves those goalposts, is simply exhausting and futile.

Don't expend energy on trying to meet these bullshit ideals. Instead, embrace your unique hotness—whether you're fat or skinny, hairy or smooth, short or tall, muscular or lean, with big hands, or small feet, or buck teeth, or freckles, or pimples. No matter what your body looks like, what shape you are, what size, what ability or mobility you have, others just like you are looking and feeling hot as fuck, and you can too!

Finding positive and affirming representation that promotes this message isn't always easy, whether we're talking about porn or pop culture or other media. Like me, you may have to look a little harder, dig a little deeper and expand outside of your regular sources to find the representation that you need to remind you that you're hot. But believe me when I say it's out there.

Reminding yourself of your hotness can help you withstand the draw of those societal ideals as a strategy for attracting a partner too. It's not worth forcing yourself into trying to meet ideals that make you feel unhappy and uncomfortable. That's not gonna sit well in the long term. It's better to embrace yourself, and do whatever you need to feel confident, attractive and good, than to mould yourself into what somebody else wants.

Instead of asking yourself, "what do I need to do in order to attract a prospective spouse or new partner?" ask, "what do I need to do in order to feel desirable and happy? And what do I need from a partner to feel safe, supported and respected?"

Remember that you're hot, and remind yourself that different types of bodies appeal to different people. And many people are indifferent to breast and genital sizes and shapes, as they value other aspects of their partners and lovers more than those parts of their bodies.

The point is that the things about your body that bring you the most insecurity are probably somebody's jam. You're a major hottie, and don't you forget it!

HETERONORMATIVITY, MARRIAGE AND FAMILY PLANNING

Meanwhile, social scripts about the paths our lives "should" take are forced onto us all the time. Especially as children, which is weird considering how much of a hot topic it is among conservatives that kids shouldn't be made aware of trans or queer identities and relationships. Meanwhile, kids' books and films depict a plethora of heterosexual romances, marriage subplots and "traditional" family units.

Just as cisnormativity keeps us locked in gendered boxes, heteronormativity works under the assumption that heterosexuality is the default, "normal" sexual orientation of all human beings, and that any deviation is somehow wrong, a mistake in need of correction. That's where films, television shows, books and school come in to show kids that they ultimately need to find their Prince Charming or their princess, the one true love they'll commit to forever, and have children with them. So much emphasis is placed on love, marriage and parenthood being our purpose in life, the main way to secure our legacy and experience true happiness and success, that choosing not to follow that path can lead to stress, anxiety, depression and low self-worth.

Once you see just how pervasive this messaging is, it's hard to unsee. And as a trans queer, it makes forging your own path, writing your own destiny, significantly more challenging and filled with hurdles.

AMATONORMATIVITY AND THE RELATIONSHIP ESCALATOR

This brings us to the concept of **amatonormativity**. Coined by philosophy professor Elizabeth Brake, the term refers to "the belief that marriage and companionate romantic love have special value," which "leads to overlooking the value of other caring relationships." It highlights the disproportionate focus on marital and romantic love relationships as being intrinsically more valuable than other connections, such as friendships or queerplatonic partnerships. She goes on to explain that the belief includes "the assumptions that a central, exclusive, amorous relationship is normal for humans, in that it is a universally shared goal, and that such a relationship is normative, in that it *should* be aimed at in preference to other relationship types."[7]

As far as the negative impact that this approach can have on your life, Brake writes, "Amatonormativity prompts the sacrifice of other relationships to romantic love and marriage and relegates friendship and solitudinousness to cultural invisibility."[8]

Basically, it's why so many of your monogamous heterosexual pals disappear out of your friendship once they start dating somebody "seriously."

By and large, we've all been conditioned to this idea that our lives aren't complete or successful unless we follow the same monolithic path of dating, love, cohabitation, proposal, marriage, homeownership, having children and retirement. All of these milestones also happen to be legally and socially most accessible to cisgender, heterosexual, nondisabled and white individuals. Journalist Amy Gahran summarizes this pretty damn succinctly in describing what she calls the **relationship escalator**:

> *"The goal at the top of the [relationship] Escalator is to achieve a permanently monogamous (sexually and romantically exclusive between two people), cohabitating marriage—legally sanctioned if possible. In many cases, buying a house and having kids is also part of the goal. Partners are expected to remain together at the top of the Escalator until death.*

---

7 Elizabeth Brake, "Amatonormativity." https://elizabethbrake.com/amatonormativity/

8 Brake, "Amatonormativity."

"The Escalator is the standard by which most people gauge whether a developing intimate relationship is significant, 'serious,' good, healthy, committed or worth pursuing or continuing."

...In other words, the Relationship Escalator is what most people grow up believing (or more accurately, assuming) that intimate relationships "should" look like, how they are "supposed" to work—and indeed, what any emotionally healthy adult "should" want.[9]

It's no wonder, then, that traditional gender roles continue to be the norm and remain difficult for people to look past. It's also no wonder that so many people who are non-white, queer, trans, disabled or otherwise different in any way often find self-acceptance and dating under these conditions to be challenging and disheartening.

WHEN AMATONORMATIVITY, THE RELATIONSHIP ESCALATOR AND RIGID GENDER NORMS MEET

Amatonormativity, heteronormativity and strict gender norms stack upon each other, and they don't just potentially hurt and stifle trans queers; they also create harmful ideals among cisgender and heterosexual folks. Lots of guys out

---

9 Amy Gahran, "What Is the Relationship Escalator?" Off the Relationship Escalator: Uncommon Love and Life. https://offescalator.com/what-escalator/.

there, for example, refuse to date women who are taller or bigger than them, not because they necessarily find these women unattractive, but because the men feel emasculated in their presence. Some guys even see these physical traits as being intrinsically masculine, not "womanly." They fear that being physically smaller than their partner will make them look, and feel, both not-heterosexual and like less of a man somehow. Unfortunately, tons of women also buy into this same ideal by refusing to date guys shorter than them. They too see height and physical build as being representative of a man's strength, prowess, sexual and reproductive ability, worth and overall masculinity. And that's honestly quite sad.

Similarly, plenty of men only pursue young women with large breasts, thin waists and "child-bearing" hips, despite how uncommon and unattainable that body is for most people. In these cases, the expectation is that a woman is only worth investing in based on her youth and ability to reproduce. These guys want the hot wife, the big expensive wedding in a church, lots of cute kids, and all of the social prestige that comes with being a "family man." The relationship escalator becomes the driving force behind all these social interactions and life decisions.

If your attractions come from a place of wanting to be bigger and stronger than your partner, or to validate your own identity to yourself or others, and if you find yourself expecting or pressuring somebody to fit your mould of what a partner "should" be, that's worth interrogating. It could be a strong sign that your attraction is based more on image than anything else, and could reflect your lack of self-confidence. A relationship does not exist for one person's sole gratification and perceived social influence or success. That's not a mutually respectful, affirming and cooperative bond.

Relationships centred on the factors I've listed here, especially those that are tied up in specific body require-ments, rarely last, and can often be harmful. By their very nature, these bonds are built upon expectations of each person remaining a certain way, which is unreasonable given that all bodies age and change as we get older. Expecting yourself to only ever have fit, young, slim people in your life because "that's who you're attracted to" is likely to leave a long wake of hurt people behind you.

And remember that if a person holds you to any of these standards and isn't going to go out with you because of your hair, piercings, identity, height, weight or any other physical reason, it's important to feel what you need to feel about it—but then let that shit go. While it always hurts to be told you're too short, or not skinny enough, don't let somebody else's hang-ups about bodies make you feel bad about yourself. And don't lament the loss of somebody who wasn't going to respect or appreciate you for who you are.

ALTERNATIVES TO MONOGAMY AND DATING NORMS (A CURSORY LOOK)

Just as you can be trans queer and express your identity in endlessly diverse ways, you can also approach dating and your relationships in endlessly diverse ways. You can choose to date a whole bunch of people and never strictly define any of those bonds, or you can develop a complex web of multiple sexual, romantic and emotional relationships with varying degrees of commitment and a mix of steps from the relationship escalator, including cohabitation or even having children. I'm not going to cover all the options here—that would be a different book!—but I encourage you to seek out information about the wide world of nonmonogamy and consider what might work best for you. Check out the resources at the back of this book for some further reading!

For example, I have been with my partner Verne since March 2020, and my husband Fenric since December 2021. Each week I go back and forth between their homes, spending a few days here and a few days there, but scheduling set date nights with both of them while also enjoying my own personal living space. Additionally, I've been privileged to enjoy meaningful relationships with satellite partners, lovers and others who have come in and out of my life and enriched it. I also get to explore nonmonogamy a fair bit in my partnerships, especially with Fenric, as we've had a few play friends with whom we've occasionally enjoyed group sex.

I've tried other relationship structures. Being strictly monogamous never worked for me and always felt like way, way too much pressure to be a partner's one and only, their "everything," all of the time. I often found myself feeling overwhelmed by being the only provider for one person's every need. But I also saw the other end of things with **relationship anarchy**, and that was too much for me. At one point in 2022, I had seven partners, three friends with benefits, and multiple play and **date friends** for casual experiences. It all fell apart quite spectacularly and many of those relationships ended.

Where I'm at now feels perfect for me. I'm in two committed relationships with my partners, Fen and Verne, that allow me space to also enjoy nonmonogamy through occasional group sex with my partners and friends, as well as the odd hookup and date with a cute trans or nonbinary queer. It's exactly what I need without risking overextending myself again. And with the many possible relationship structures available, you can find something that feels perfect for you too. The key to polyamory being ethical is that everyone knows what's going on and consents to it, and everyone's feelings are considered. I don't suddenly start new relationships or have impromptu hookups without first having thorough conversations with my partners, and I always put **safer sex** practices firmly in place. If you're secretly sleeping with a bunch of people while telling each partner that they're your one and only, that's not polyamory—it's cheating.

So, if you're going to explore polyamory and nonmonogamy, be sure to do some more reading!

IT'S NOT YOU, IT'S THEM

The world around us is not exactly supportive or encouraging of thinking outside norms. But I hope that these first few chapters have shown that while you can certainly take steps to find your sexy and to forge the trans queer–affirming bonds you want, much of the struggle you've experienced—internal, external or both—comes not from you but from an extremely powerful and determined culture clinging onto patriarchal and religious traditions above all else. For the fiftieth time (OK, I haven't actually been keeping count): no wonder us trans queers often don't know how to feel sexy, find the connections we desire or even fully realize ourselves most of the time!

You're not failing. It's not your fault if you're feeling a lot of bad things about yourself or your body. Those negative thoughts come from all of the messaging we've been hearing our whole lives. The rest of this book focuses on advice and guidance for ways you can feel better in your identity, find your sexual self and feel hotter in the process. As you read on, remember that if people aren't celebrating your self-exploration and identity, it's not you...it's them.

CHAPTER 6
GET YOUR SEXY ON

Time for some practical guidance and tips on putting your look together in ways that feel affirming and empowering! We've spent a great deal of time talking about what we find sexy in others, both personal traits and overall vibes. And we have explored how sexy can feel in terms of our emotional wellness, comfort, safety and euphoria about being trans queer and being seen in the ways that feel most affirming. But sometimes it also feels nice to *look* sexy!

For some, looking sexy might be about finding partners or lovers, or feeling desired by others and receiving compliments. For others, it may be a way to improve their confidence and feel good about how they're expressing themselves to the world. Both perspectives are valid, and there are many ways to express yourself as a trans queer in any environment, whether you're at school, at work, at home, out running errands or, yes, in the bedroom with people you fancy. It's OK to want to look good in a way that feels good to you, regardless of intent!

I'm gonna preface the rest of this chapter by saying that the most important aspect of exploring what feels sexy for you is going to be your comfort and willingness to experiment. It might take a bunch of trial and error for you to find what approach works best when it comes to physically expressing yourself. You may discover things that feel very good right now, but that might change a few times over the coming weeks, months or years. But that's OK! We all grow and change, and none of those changes invalidate who you are. Shifting how you express yourself, changing your labels, trying out different words and pronouns—it's all OK, no matter how many times you do it, or for whatever reasons. Fear about our validity as trans queers is pretty common, given how much we're questioned about who we are. But don't let that fear keep you from seeking new ways of being, and don't allow anyone to guilt, pressure or shame you out of dressing and expressing yourself how you want to.

Also, please know that you can try whatever you like. Even if a style or vibe seems like it's more typically masculine or feminine, you're totally allowed to get creative and reconstruct it to fit your individuality better. There are no rules about what you can and can't wear based on what pronouns you use or what genitals you have, and you're free to explore your self-expression however you wish, despite how some styles may typically be worn. Nothing is truly gender locked, and your body doesn't disqualify you from wearing any type of clothing or enjoying any aesthetic.

Whatever your body may look like, whatever your build may be, you can and should express yourself in the ways that make you feel good and excited. Be sure to keep this point in mind over the course of the chapter as we look at the myriad ways you can physically affirm your identity and prepare yourself for potential wardrobe growth. We'll also go over some of the well-known styles and forms of self-expression that are seen across many trans queer communities, which you can try on for yourself!

TRANS QUEER-AFFIRMING PROSTHETICS AND MORE

Luckily for trans queer folks, the market has made leaps and bounds in terms of providing affirming prosthetics, enhancers, shapers and beyond. For a flatter chest, try binders or TransTape. For a curvier form, consider shaping slips, shorts, leggings or bodysuits, as well as control briefs, corsets and waist cinchers. For a nice little bulge, check out packers. For a hard dick, there are ultra-realistic cocks, dildos, stand-to-pee devices and more. For larger or fuller breasts, try wearable breast forms or moulds, push-up bras or bustiers.

Whether you're preparing for a night of intimacy, going out on a date, socializing with friends or heading off to work, you are absolutely within your rights to put on whatever you need to feel better. Do it for the positive attention, or do it for yourself! Both choices are valid. I strongly encourage you to express yourself in whatever ways make you feel most euphoric, regardless of whether the environment you'll be in is professional, social, casual or intimate.

And never forget that when you're in a sexual situation, you never have to be fully naked, or use any specific part of your body for sex, if you don't want to. Keep the binder on, don't take off the panties, wear your shirt the whole time if you want to. You're going to feel your sexiest when you're most comfortable.

A LACK OF TRANS-INCLUSIVE LINGERIE AND UNDERWEAR

Whether you identify as trans, genderqueer, a cross-dresser, a drag performer, whatever, it can unfortunately be a pretty uphill battle to find clothing, especially lingerie, that fits. You'll see an incredibly wide array of bras, panties, corsets, nighties, teddys, bodysuits, camisoles, bustiers, slips, stockings and more to choose from out there, but almost none of them are created with trans queer bodies in mind.

As a trans queer person with a penis, I've personally found this challenge most noticeable when it comes to panties. All of the best cutesy, frilly, lacey, silky panties are created for cis women and are pretty inaccessible to those of us who don't have the narrow range of bodies that manufacturers have decided to cater to. These design choices leave a lot of people out, including cis women who are larger or who have disabilities.

Even when panties are designed for people other than women, it's perplexing that they tend to be marketed almost exclusively to cishet men and queer men. Which...why?

At its core, this situation is part of a major cisnormativity problem that Cora Harrington of *The Lingerie Addict* has touched on a number of times in her writing. "A trans woman friend I asked broke lingerie into three categories: primarily designed for cisgender women, primarily designed for people into 'being feminized' as a fetish or a punishment, or 'well-intentioned' transgender-specific options," Cora explained in a 2014 post that specifically addressed the issues of cis men–centric lingerie shops and the exclusion of trans people from consideration in this retail space. "Men who crossdress get all this beautiful lingerie to choose from at a range of price points, including whole lines specifically designed to fit their bodies that still [validate] their masculine gender identities—and trans women have to either fit themselves into clothes designed with cisgender women's bodies in mind, or resign themselves to buying lingerie marketed with hairy male models and large text declaring that this stuff is *for men*."[10]

I think Harrington is onto some pretty big things here, and I feel that good business sense includes the ability to research and learn about other demographics to expand your business and create a more comfortable and inclusive experience for your clientele. It's needlessly limiting and unfortunate to use strictly gendered marketing that caters exclusively to cisgender and heterosexual dudes when your products also have wide appeal for trans queer folks. It's not overly difficult to consult trans people and nonbinary folks, in addition to cis queers, to make your shop more accessible and enticing to a broader clientele outside of binary cishets. In fact, it can be as simple as using more inclusive language and addressing trans queer folks in your advertising.

Until the day when traditional retailers consider trans queers in their marketing and products, your best bet to find affirming shopping experiences is to seek out smaller niche stores hosted through online markets like Etsy. In

---

10 Cora Harrington, "Where Is the Lingerie for Trans Women?" *The Lingerie Addict*, November 11, 2014. https://www.thelingerieaddict. com/2014/11/lingerie-trans-women.html.

these specialty spaces, you're more likely to find trans queer lingerie made by other trans queers, or at least by people who have actually consulted trans queers. It's a pretty jarring difference to see after looking at the more mainstream stores, where we're not even an afterthought.

However, prices at these smaller niche retailers can be a little steep at times, and buying online may not be accessible for everyone. If you want to find panties as a person with a penis, but you need to do so at the bigger shops, either online or in person, don't panic—I have a lot of experience with this process and I'm going to tell you what I've learned.

First, breathe! If you're like me and used to wear basic boxers, briefs and boxer briefs, shopping for panties can be super overwhelming at first. They come in a ridiculous number of types and fits. Not a couple options—a lot. Way more than you would think are necessary. You can find boy shorts, hip-huggers, cheekies, bikinis, thongs, high-cuts, high-waists, tangas, hipsters, classic briefs, control briefs and a bajillion types of "strings"—and they all differ further in fabric and style from retailer to retailer. This variety gets frustrating when you find a type that you really like...only to realize that not all brands make that style the same way, so you either need to stick to the same manufacturer (hoping they don't discontinue what you like) or constantly shift between styles and sizing from shop to shop.

If you tuck, assessing comfort and aesthetics with different styles and sizes may be more straightforward as you won't have to account for penis room. But if you're like me and mostly wear panties casually, or to feel comfortable and cute, or to feel sexy with your penis untucked, it's important to research all of the aforementioned styles to see which may be best for your bits! Just understand that you may still go through some trial and error no matter how prepared you are.

Whether it's for day-to-day wear or for sexytimes, I find that getting a slightly larger size than I need makes for a more comfortable wear without my cock being so smooshed that it uncomfortably turtles itself into my pubic mound. The snugger your panties are, the more likely your penis is going to tuck its damn self whether you want it to or not, especially when you factor in other layers of tight clothing and the shifting that occurs throughout the day.

Now, I'm not talking about going to a 2XL if you normally wear a small, but giving yourself slightly more room can help quite a bit, so long as your panties aren't falling off your hips. I can fit a size large in many brands of panties, but since I started buying size XL, my genitals have thanked me for all the extra comfort room and I'm adjusting myself far less throughout the day.

Once you have a pair of panties to try, it's time to play with your penis...positioning-wise, that is! What works best for me in an upsized pair of panties is to just place my penis all the way to one side to rest nicely cradled in the fabric. From there, I can gauge how comfortable the panties are going to be for me in the long term. In the right pair, like a roomy hipster fit or a nice XL lace cheeky, my penis (while flaccid or even partially erect) sits comfortably without turtling itself or poking out noticeably from underneath the fabric. However, if the pair I'm wearing is a little tight, I find it's better for me to position my cock upright and slightly to the side so the head is pointing just off-centre of my belly button at a two o'clock or 10 o'clock position. This fit isn't ideal, but I can still make it work for myself if I like the patterns or feel of the panties and want to wear them on occasion.

Some types of panties are a lot harder to wear with an untucked penis. Most thongs and G-strings just don't have a lot of fabric, so if you're wearing them, know that you may pop out a lot, especially during any sexy or intimate times when you're more likely to become aroused.

I know it's a lot to think about, but trust me, it's worth it. While it may seem like you'll never find a pair that feels good for you, I assure you that with patience—and a whole lot of experimentation—you'll eventually find the right fit and maker for you.

BOXERS AND BRIEFS: SHOPPING TIPS FOR PEOPLE WITH A VULVA

While panties may not have been designed with penises in mind, making them difficult for penis-havers to shop for, boxes and briefs were. Which is great! Except, of course, if you don't have one. Almost all briefs and boxer briefs come with that little bit of extra fabric up front, known as the joey pouch, to hold a penis and testicles. So whereas I often recommend buying panties a size up for more penis room, with boxers and briefs, it may be worth going down a size if you can. While sizing down may make your briefs feel a little uncomfortable due to a tighter band and leg holes, it also means a smaller joey pouch to bunch up awkwardly in the front of your pants or dangle out in front of you while you're lounging at home. Another option is to focus on finding yourself some nice boxers, which have an open or buttoned fly, without the pouch, though sometimes this style can be harder to find on store shelves.

Some basic, affordable brands also offer no-fly and "breathable" alternatives, which are generally less loose up front. My husband Fenric is pretty small all around, so he just buys boys' boxer briefs because they fit much better and don't typically have a joey pouch, which helps. Some of my other partners have preferred basic briefs, as they can be quite breathable and cozy overall. If you intend to use a packer, choose underwear with adequate dick room for it.

Should you have a bit more flexibility in your finances, you may want to look into specialty trunks, boxers and briefs made for trans people. These include specifically designed packing underwear, boxers with O-rings and built-in harnesses, and masculine-styled period underwear for people who menstruate with an extra panel to hold store-bought pads. Take the time to look around, read trans queer forums and see what other folks seem to be buying and recommending!

GET YOUR MEASUREMENTS RIGHT

One of the biggest mistakes I've ever made while shopping for myself was doing so without having taken proper measurements for my body. I had become so accustomed to just knowing whether I was a medium, large or XL in a particular brand that I never considered the fact that my body had dimensions to it. Knowing those numbers has allowed me to buy clothing that fits me properly, and has helped me feel more attractive and empowered.

Taking your measurements includes a lot of steps, but while it may feel like overkill at first, you'll be glad you did it—especially when it comes time to buy specialty items, such as jewelry, headpieces, lingerie and kink/fetish gear.

Be sure to use a measuring tape that doesn't stretch at all. Cloth tape is great, but be aware that it does stretch over time, so if you have had yours for quite a while, it would be a good idea to replace it. Ideally, you'll want somebody else to take these measurements for you, as doing it yourself creates a higher chance of inaccuracies. Also, try not to take your measurements while wearing bulky clothing of any kind. Get down to your underwear, if possible!

Be sure to record your measurements in both centimetres and inches, to save you from making conversations later if retailers only list one type of product measurements. If you plan to shop online, it would be beneficial to write down the specific sizes you buy in Canada, the United States, United Kingdom, France, Australia, China, Japan, South Korea or any other nations from which you purchase. Different countries use different size-numbering systems; sizing practices are not standard across the world. A size 10 men's shoe in Canada and the United States is a 9 in the United Kingdom and Australia, a 28 in Japan and a 280 in South Korea. Similarly, the United States and United Kingdom have bra cup sizes ranging from as small as AA to as large as J, and specialty shops may offer an even wider array, whereas other nations, such as China and France, typically only go up to an E or F.

The Disabled World community has compiled an extensive page of charts comparing international sizing for various types of clothing, which can be helpful as you shop online.[11]

Shopping can be especially challenging if your body is different in any way from those of companies' standard fit models. A lot of clothes aren't designed with diverse bodies in mind, including bodies that are curvy, large, super petite, tall or short. While North American retailers typically offer sizes from XS up to XXXL, and possibly larger, many international companies have narrower production around diversity in clothing. A lack of inclusive design makes finding things to feel sexy in an especially challenging and frustrating experience. But it's worth the effort to search for what you desire!

The body measurements you need depend largely on the types of garments you're shopping for. In some cases, you may be able to hold an item up to your body and get a decent sense of whether or not it will fit, but that requires you to feel comfortable shopping openly for items that staff and other shoppers may react to seeing you interacting with. If you don't feel safe doing that out in the open, some stores provide dressing rooms for you to try on garments before purchasing them. Having a friend come with you to carry items for you, or bring them to you to try on, may relieve a lot of stress as it provides a sort of disconnect between you and the clothing you wish to try on until you are able to interact with it more privately. If you plan to

---

11 Disabled World, "Male and Female Clothing Size Conversion Charts." Updated September 16, 2023. https://www.disabled-world. com/calculators-charts/clothing-sizes.php.

shop mainly in person, knowing your measurements isn't entirely necessary. However, if you're ordering online, or having anything custom made for you from a specialty shop, it may be necessary to get a wide range of measurements.

Luckily, it's all pretty straightforward, so let's just go through the typical measurements one by one. All you'll need is your flexible tape measure, be it cloth or another kind of body measuring tape, and a way to record your results. As you measure, do your best to ensure that you're not pulling the tape too tight, and take each measurement a few times to ensure your numbers are as accurate as possible.

Head: Make sure that the measuring tape starts at the middle of your forehead, then stays level as it wraps around your head. It should sit slightly above your ears and at the midway point between the back of your neck and crown of your head. Finding your head measurement will help you pick out hats, headbands, tiaras, crowns and other head accessories.

Neck: Place the measuring tape about an inch above where the base of your neck meets your collar, and carefully wrap it around your neck from this point. This number will help you with necklaces, collars, chokers and some types of shirts and other tops.

Chest: Wrap the measuring tape around the fullest part of your chest, under your armpits, at nipple level.

Bust: This measurement should be done on bare breasts and can be taken in three key steps. Firstly, while standing, loosely wrap the measuring tape around your torso and breasts at the fullest part, like the chest measurement above. Next, bend over at 90 degrees and do the same, measuring loosely around the fullest part of your bust. Finally, while lying on your back, once again measure loosely around the fullest part of your chest. It may help to have someone else aid you with doing these measurements, or even just reading your results. For more guidance on getting accurate measurements of your bust, visit abrathatfits.org and its forum at reddit.com/r/abrathatfits. You can enter these three measurements (plus the band measurements you'll take next) into the calculator on abrathatfits.org to see recommended bra sizes.

Band: To get this measurement, be sure to not wear a bra, or at least wear one without padding. Wrap the measuring tape around your chest just under your breasts, where a bra band would sit. While you should have the measuring tape relatively snug against your body, leave a finger's width worth of space between it and your body so that you're not pulling too tight, which could result in a too-tight bra band.

Wrist: Open your hand and rotate it so your palm is facing up. This position means your wrist is at its most flexed and widest. Place the end of your measuring tape in the middle of your wrist, then wrap it around and back to the starting position. This measurement is handy for bracelets, watches, bangles and cuffs, and may be needed for some shirts, especially fitted or tailored ones.

Waist: Place the end of the measuring tape just above your belly button, then wrap it around your torso. A waist measurement is great info for buying body and waist harnesses, corsets, cinchers and the like! It may also be useful for purchasing pants and belts, much like the next measurement.

Hip: Stand up straight with your feet pointed straight ahead. Wrap your measuring tape around the widest, fullest part of your hips, which includes going around your butt.

Thigh: While standing up straight, make sure your weight is evenly distributed between your feet. Place the end of your measuring tape on the midway point between your hip and kneecap, then wrap it around your thigh. This number will help you pick out comfortable thigh harnesses and strap-ons, and also figure out the right fit for specialty underwear, tall boots and thigh-high socks.

Calf: As when measuring your thighs, make sure your feet are planted flat on the floor and wrap the measuring tape around the widest part of your calf. This measurement can be particularly useful when buying knee-high and thigh-high socks, as well as tall boots.

Ankle: Find your ankle bone and wrap the tape measure around your leg at that point. This measurement will be useful for finding anklets that fit, and may be necessary for some types of pants.

Foot: The easiest method for getting an accurate foot size is to go to a shoe store to have your measurements taken with a Brannock device. Most staff members can help you use the device, though you're certainly allowed to request to do it on your own. If visiting a store isn't an option, you'll get a more or less accurate number by placing your foot on a white piece of paper and tracing around it. Then measure the distance between your heel and longest toe with a ruler. You can then take that number and consult The Disabled World's size conversion charts to figure out what size shoes will work for you.

While the above measurements can help cover a lot of the more standard purchasing needs, you may require some more precise numbers if you're having something custom made, such as a tailored suit or commissioned fursuit, or even some particularly unique specialty dresses, gowns and fetish gear. Below, you'll find a handful of those more niche measurements and how to take them.

Shoulder: You'll likely need some help with taking this measurement, as it's difficult to do accurately on your own. Stand with your back straight, but your shoulders relaxed. Unlike other measurements, your shoulders can be measured from the front or back. When measuring from the back, have your helper measure from one shoulder point to the other (not from your arms), along the natural curve of your body. Instead of pulling the measuring tape taut, let it follow your shoulder slightly up and across the base of the back of your neck. From the front, you'll also measure from your shoulder points, but you'll spread the measuring tape in a straight line across the front of your collarbones instead.

Torso: This one is also much easier with a helper. Wrap the measuring tape fully around your torso, starting from where your shoulder meets your neck, then down and across the fullest part of your chest/bust, then down between your legs and between your butt cheeks before looping around back to the starting point.

Torso length: Keep your helper with you! Have them place the end of the measuring tape at the base of the back of your neck and follow the curve of your spine down to your waist. To help mark exactly where your waist is, place both of your hands over your hip bones. Record the distance between the base of your neck and your waist.

Arm: Starting at the nape of your neck, run your tape measure in a straight line over your shoulder and all the way down your arm to your wrist.

Outer leg to hem: Starting from your waist, measure down your leg to wherever your preferred length of pants would sit. This measurement may differ depending on the shoes you plan to wear with different pants. For example, you'll likely want longer pants if you are planning on wearing heels, so you may want to take this measurement a couple of times wearing different types of shoes.

Inner leg (inseam): Place the end of the measuring tape as close to your crotch as is comfortable, and measure down the inside of your leg to where the hem of your pants would sit.

Now that you've got your measurements, you'll be prepared to make informed decisions about your next purchase or clothing swap find. You may want to retake your measurements once a year, or anytime you change size in some way (weight gain or loss, surgery, becoming more muscular, or other kinds of changes) to make sure they're up to date before you spend money on garments. Remember, these numbers are to help you get clothing that feels and looks good. They provide you with information—and big or small, they're not a value judgment!

WHERE TO BEGIN

The thing about wearing stuff that makes you feel sexy is that there's a vast array of possibilities, and almost anything can be sexy in the right context.

Getting started can be pretty overwhelming, especially if you're coming into this whole process with a lot of uncertainty about what you're looking for. I know that when I first came out as trans queer, the entire concept of what was sexy and attractive for me was pretty nonexistent. I didn't tend to think a lot about how I looked and gravitated toward wearing oversized hoodies, baggy jeans and large graphic T-shirts. Everything I put on was at least one or two sizes too big for my body. In retrospect, I think I basically wanted to be covered up and barely perceived. I wanted to feel comfortable, but not exactly noticeable, and I hated putting much thought into my self-expression. In all honesty, I barely remember how I appeared in my teens and throughout my twenties, as I barely recall looking at myself in the mirror.

So, prior to coming out, feeling sexy was never a thing I thought about for myself. Shifting into exploring my sexuality and body as a trans queer was confusing, because I didn't have the cishet experience of expressing myself in an empowering way. I was completely lost and had no idea where to even start. It wasn't until I started seeing other trans queers in my community, and online through blogging and social media, that I finally started to envision what might work for me.

At first, I figured that if I was sexually attracted to a person based on how they looked, then dressing that same way would likely make me feel sexy too. Right? I mean, logically it made sense to me that the styles, vibes and looks of trans queers I was attracted to would likely feel good for me as well. That wasn't always the case, though... especially because in a lot of instances, I was seeing specific styles on specific body types, namely thin femboys or AFAB individuals dressed alternatively queer. Based on what I was seeing, none of those styles seemed like they were made for bodies like my own. Even at my smallest, I was still a short, stocky, hairy person with broad shoulders, a big chest, thick thighs and a pretty bodacious booty. With my physical traits, trying to shop for femboy-style clothing, or even casual femme wear, was exceedingly challenging and depressing. A lot of these clothing items, especially dresses and bras, weren't made with my body in mind.

At several points over the course of a decade, I fell into a tailspin, feeling unattractive with my wardrobe and unable to find what I wanted to wear in sizes that fit. The more I struggled to find clothing I was excited about in my size, the worse I felt and the more I worried that I'd never be able to express myself in the ways I really wanted to. I even just gave up a few times, falling back to my old habits of relying on baggy pants, oversized sweaters and too-big graphic T-shirts. That wardrobe was my coping space. The thing is, it didn't actually help at all. I was basically just denying myself any effort to find my sexy self, while wallowing in a defeatist attitude that was basically "nothing fits me and I don't look good in most styles, so why bother?"

Ultimately, I had to let go of trying to be too exact in replicating what I saw other cute trans queers doing and forge a look that's entirely my own. It's taken many, many years of trial and error, of sadness and overwhelm, but I feel like I'm more on track now. The trick was leaning into the fact that no one style was working for me, so the answer was to just do whatever the fuck I wanted with all of them. Most of what makes me feel attractive now incorporates a mixture of elements found in dapper queer styles, '90s grunge rock, witchy gay vibes, **campy** bear aesthetics and a healthy dash of sexy librarian. And hey, if none of those terms sound familiar to you, don't worry, we'll be diving into them all shortly!

A key step for me was finding staple items that felt good, and then building up from there. My absolute must-have items of clothing are cute patterned leggings, a range of black skirts of various lengths, basic black or grey tank tops, and a handful of flattering dresses (skater and summer dresses tend to look great on my fabulously fat body). From that base, I'm able to mix and match additional items, bring in fun accessories, and buy new tops, shoes and other articles of clothing that I can either combine with the stuff I already have or use to build a whole new outfit.

The process of building a wardrobe that I feel great in was very slow, and it's still ongoing today as I continue to learn about what makes me feel attractive and empowered. So if you're finding the very idea of finding your look to be challenging or overwhelming, please don't worry! It can take a lot of time for some folks, and at some points, you may feel a little worse before you feel better. But the work is worth it! If I were to give you one major piece of advice, it's this: pay attention to your feelings and respect your body. Don't try to force something on yourself that makes you feel bad, even if you really want it to make you feel good. Don't let resentment fester if things don't work out exactly like you hoped. Be kind and patient with yourself. Be accommodating to your body and don't punish yourself for the unrealistic body ideals and standards held by so many. If an article of clothing isn't working for you, or maybe a whole vibe you liked isn't clicking, it's OK to mourn that a little, but don't let it spoil your whole journey.

And there's no rush with this process! Feel free to take your time, especially in the beginning, to allow yourself room to just explore and experiment. Like me, you may be able to find a lot of inspiration by paying attention to the trans queers you see online and in your friend circles or local community. You can also look to the many trans and nonbinary queer performers, artists, content creators and creatives expressing themselves on film, television and all over social media nowadays. Additionally, for the nerdy gamers out there, many games now employ detailed character creators with a surprising number of customization options. Using these tools to visualize hairstyles, tattoos, piercings and even outfit concepts for yourself can work wonders and help you think creatively about what would make you feel good.

In my own exploration, I used a personal blog and various social media platforms to connect with others, find inspiration and share my own journey. These channels allowed me to go back through pictures of my various outfits and to reflect on how they made me feel. The looks I liked became beacons for how I'd move forward, while those that didn't quite work, or made me feel insecure, served as reminders for what to avoid. If that's something that interests you, I recommend using online space to catalogue your experiences along the way. However, you can also use a notebook or journal, or even create a scrapbook of selfies, pictures, magazine clippings, printouts and more for consideration. Be sure to also make notes of what feelings each image evokes, good and bad, and pay close attention to those feelings—they're important!

With all of these considerations in mind, I'd like to share with you some of the styles and aesthetics that have jumped out to me personally over the years. This is not an exhaustive list; it's more of a selection of the vast range of styles out there, and of course I've focused on some of the ones I like best. Queer and trans people are often very creative, and we have a long history of being at the leading edge of fashion and style, so in our communities, change and innovation are constant.

I hope something here inspires you! If one or more of these styles resonates with you, I hope this section might also give you some keywords to consider while searching for outfit ideas online or connecting with groups of people who appreciate the same styles as you. Also bear in mind that the best part of a look is *you*, so don't feel you need to conform to any one rigid style. It's great to mix and match and put your personal touch on any look you create.

BUTCH QUEER

Butch is typically more of an identity than a style, and it's associated with a broad range of fashion choices, from the more casual tank tops and comfy shorts to more formal attire with suits, ties, dress shirts, blazers and the like. Overall, butch folks take on the clothing styles that have often been associated with and even "reserved" for cis men, dating back to when AFAB people could not even wear pants without causing a stir, and pushing back against the gender roles and expectations that have limited self-expression for so long. Butchness also has roots deep within feminism, within empowerment of a spectrum of AFAB and queer people, and of being able to safely wear what one feels most comfortable in.

Nobody has been able to pin down exactly when the term "butch" entered the queer lexicon, but its early usage in the 1940s and '50s typically described gender expressions in lesbian culture that were far more masculine than feminine, beyond even what some might consider a **tomboy**. A lot of butch women frequented dyke bars, where their overall aesthetic was strongly influenced by working-class men and their vibe leaned heavily into subverting masculinity by embodying aspects of it while simultaneously meshing it with their own individual take on queer sexuality. It wasn't just about looking more masculine, though; being butch meant incorporating and challenging the social role of men within the context of lesbian identity and relationships.

The butch-femme relationship structure caused a lot of uproar throughout the 1940s and 1950s (and still does today for some cishet people and anti-queer groups) for daring to inhabit the same space as cishet folks. In these lesbian couples, one partner was more masculine and took on a lot of the roles, responsibilities and expectations typically reserved for cis men. And that's where butches especially shined! Their very existence provoked and threatened people who believed in traditional relationship and family structures, simply by suggesting that queer women didn't need cis men to fill those traditional roles; they could do so themselves and with each other.

Some people suggest that being butch is often the precursor to many individuals later discovering they are in fact trans men, nonbinary or gender nonconforming. While there is certainly some truth to this path, in that for some people, exploring butch expression can lead to further revelations about gender, being butch doesn't inherently make someone trans or nonbinary. That being said, many gender-diverse folks have embraced being butch on their own terms and made it entirely their own thing. It helps that since the turn of the millennium, as masculinity has been influenced more and more by LGBTQ+ individuals, it allows for a ton of unique expression that can include aspects of historical queer butchness alongside a more modern approach, and can involve as much or as little androgyny or femininity as you'd like.

DAPPER QUEER

Aesthetically speaking, dapper style can involve a lot of crossover with butch aesthetics, but the distinction lies in the fact that the dapper queer has no degree of casual wear. This look is far more focused on style than on identity. This whole aesthetic is about masculine (and androgynous) queer formality mixed with vibrant elegance to create a gender-nonconforming handsome look.

Regardless of how you identify, you can be dapper as fuck if you'd like! The dapper look leans heavily into adopting dressy masculine styles gleaned from various points in history and accentuates them with more modern vibrance in brighter and richer colours outside of the basic browns, blacks, whites and greys typically associated with formalwear. Some dapper queers gravitate toward the roaring '20s and speakeasy aesthetics, while others vibe more in timeless '50s, swinging '60s, disco '70s or even yuppie '80s styles. The general idea is to recreate masculine formal looks with modern kicks. Dapper style takes all of those traditional concepts of fancy dress and businessman attire and radicalizes them with bold patterns, shades, textures and fits.

Many dapper queers make it a goal to not only look amazing, but also to actively destabilize and push social boundaries around formality. If ever you run into heavily gendered workplace dress codes or social expectations around professional appearances, you can expect a dapper queer to be there, looking so fucking cool in the most nonconforming way they possibly can.

FEMBOYS

Femboys are an interesting bunch because though many dress cute and femme, they still identify as boys and may or may not consider themselves part of the trans queer community. While this tends to be an individual choice in my experience, I've also sadly seen a great deal of hostility toward femboys by trans queer folks who don't seem to like or support them for weirdly gatekeeping and often transphobic reasons. It's disappointing to see, especially considering that a number of femboys are also trans men, trans women and enbies. A blanket view that any particular identity is "not trans enough" harms a lot of younger trans queers, including those who haven't come out yet. Like crossdressers before them, femboys tend to get a lot of shit for "performative queerness," which is hot garbage, and I love to see how many of them lean into their desires even more aggressively to counter that hostility.

What I've always found most impressive is that femboys have one of the most distinctive and well-realized looks and communities out there. Staples of the femboy look include: solid white and/or black thigh-highs, garters (especially leather), skirts (pleated and plaid—anything to show off the thighs), slightly oversized long-sleeved sweaters, crop tops, hoodies, maid outfits, sporty shorts, arm warmers, fingerless gloves, cat ears and tails, energy drinks and a large variety of cutesy things. And don't forget Blåhaj the Ikea shark and other plushies! Soft, comfy companions are the femboys' best friend.

In lewd posting spaces, especially on Twitter (now known as X, a platform that may cease to exist, thanks to owner Elon Musk), femboys take a delightfully subversive approach to expressing their sexuality and gender and building community. Everything they post is designed to undermine and challenge gender roles and expectations, while also, ideally, making even the most conservative-minded of readers feel some degree of gay crisis as they question their own attractions. Femboys are all about radical queerness and destabilizing traditional ideals around self-identity using their greatest assets: memes, cat-boy-maid outfits, the ability to crush energy drink cans between their supple thighs, and their visibly tight buttholes and, oftentimes, shockingly large dicks.

TRANS QUEER PUNK

By its very nature, punk is a radical, nonconforming movement and style born from antiestablishment ideologies and a desire for individual freedom, which makes it a natural draw for trans queers. Since it fully took hold in the United Kingdom during the '70s, punk has always been about loudly and aggressively challenging authority and the status quo, and it continues to do so today. In its best iterations, punk also opposes bigotry, subjugation, rigid traditionalism and cops (because **ACAB**), and it strongly encourages the punching of Nazis, as should every movement.

You always know when a punk is in the room. Unlike most everyone else dressed in casual clothing or business attire, the punk strides in with their torn clothes, brightly coloured and partially shaved hair, and loud, clomping, often studded Doc Martens. Nothing about their look says "store-bought" because in addition to being antiestablishment, tired of being tied down by government overreach and rigid social norms, punks are also anti-capitalist and hate the idea of mass-produced identity. As such, their attire is often mostly thrifted, and if it does come from more commercial shelves, it's always drastically altered and defaced to undermine the original marketing or material design. Clothing is all customized, cut, slashed, patched and stitched together in a Frankenstein manner to shock, awe and upset the masses. It's all about disruption. A punk *wants* to roll eyes, turn heads and hear the grumpy groans of traditional-minded folks.

Some trans queer punks also take this aesthetic and further subvert the hell out of it by loudly fucking around with nonconforming gender expression, queer sexuality and even the expectations around gender and sexuality within punk culture itself. While punk scenes can sometimes be quite heteronormative and cisnormative, many are becoming much less so, as sexually and gender-diverse folks are increasingly drawn to this subculture due to shared values of individuality and resistance. It's a natural fit for trans queers who don't want to conform and are invested in challenging both their oppression and oppressors in their day-to-day lives. I mean, just think about our responses to rigid gender roles and expectations. Many of us reject these expectations and insist on existing as our authentic selves despite increased violent pushback from society. If that's not punk as fuck, I don't know what else could be.

The decorative choices of trans queer punks additionally bring in a lot of explicitly queer imagery, slogans, nudity, and pro-abortion, body-positive, sex-positive and anti-racist messaging in addition to the regular anti-religious and anti-facist imagery already common in punk culture. You're also bound to see significantly more vocal rhetoric against police violence and oppression due to the long history of queerphobic and transphobic policing practices in various regions.

For punks, the movement and its expression have always been quite provocative, and in many instances the body itself is seen as in opposition to the world. Punks spit in the face of society, challenging what society defines and polices as "normal" and "acceptable" ways for people to exist. And many trans queer punks seek to further radicalize the radical and burn all that is wrong with the world down to the ground. In many ways, queer punk is punk extra!

Nikki Hearts and Rizzo Ford star in
Crash Pad Series **"Episode 164."**

KITTENS, PUPS AND OTHER PETS

Probably my personal favourite style realm is that of pet- and animal-like accessories. While it may seem like these items are only for people into pet play and ownership kinks, they also lend themselves really well to just about any look, and you don't have to incorporate them in any particularly intimate way outside of just enjoying the aesthetic. In fact, kitten, pup and other animal looks are not so much stand-alone styles as they are add-ons that complement other aesthetics. You can basically add ears and tails to any gender expression along the vast spectrum of transness and it's going to be real heckin' cute.

For example, you could embrace a soft, femme, pink-adorned kitten look, with lots of lace trim, silk ribbons, bows, white cotton thigh-highs and bubblegum-coloured ears. Or maybe you're an emo, moody, sad cat femboy with oversized dark hoodies, black studded collars, pleated skirts, and gothic-style garters and thigh harnesses. Perhaps you're very twinky and take to being a pup, complete with droopy ears, chest harnesses, leather paw gloves, tank tops and booty shorts. Basically, anyone can be a kitten, pup or other pet, and adding this transformative, fantastical element to your style can be a lot of fun.

Etsy features plenty of pet-gear shops, and sellers at various conventions and events within and adjacent to nerdy communities make a wide range of incredible tails, ears, collars, cuffs, paws and more. Many creators also sell these items in matching sets, such as ears and a tail, and you can add them to any outfit to kick up the cuteness or playful factor. Ears are also quite popular on their own, and you can get a wide range of different types: cats or kittens, dogs or pups, wolves, foxes, mice, rabbits or bunnies, cows, and even deer, often with accompanying antlers.

Many people use pet accessories to embrace and accentuate aspects of their personality. Those who lean into pup vibes tend to be playful, energetic, curious, excitable and even very submissive. Some people may even want to role-play as a pup to some degree, whether it's making barking and whining sounds while being playful and cuddly, or being in a relationship dynamic in which their Master has collared and named them. A pup might also enjoy it when their Master bathes them, plays with them, and trains them to do tricks and follow obedience instructions. Kittens, meanwhile, tend to be sweet, soft, affectionate and maybe even a little aloof, though a lot of bratty folks tend to gravitate to being kittens. Like with pups, kittens may also have an ownership dynamic. Most of the kittens I know value being praised, worshipped, treated and cared for in myriad emotional and physical ways, including being groomed, fed, cuddled and pampered.

While it's not in my own wheelhouse, there's also pony play, which appeals to a noteworthy community of people. Pony gear typically involves full-body leather suits with leather horse-head hoods, a smaller custom saddle, a bit, and hooved gloves and boots. I've even seen folks who have access to a farm go out into a horse corral to do a pony show sort of play with partners, and I think that's pretty cool!

Beyond pups, kittens and ponies, you'll find wild-pet play, which is a whole category of its own involving animals that aren't typically domesticated. It includes people who play as wolves, foxes, cows, deer, bears, otters and more. In some cases, partners might also play out a predator-and-prey dynamic together.

Remember that while these descriptions of pups, kittens and other animals may inspire you or guide you toward the looks, relationships and dynamics that you desire, there are no hard rules. You are free to subvert expectations and take up elements of these styles in your own unique way, whether you just enjoy the pet and animal aesthetics or want to include aspects of sexual play. You don't have to fully invest, either—you can certainly wear cat ears and a tail just for fun!

Beau Bug and Cosmo Bug star in *Crash Pad Series* **"Episode 369".**

FURRIES AND FURSUITERS

Some folks who are into pet play might also cross over into the furry community. The two aren't inherently tied together, though! Unlike most pet players, furries go the extra mile and create anthropomorphic animal characters they relate to, inhabit or role-play. A character like this is referred to as a **fursona**. A person might explore their self-perception, and sometimes their sexuality, through their fursona. Or they might just enjoy drawing their fursona or commissioning art that features it as a cool original character.

Some furries build their own **fursuit** designed to look like their fursona, or commission one from one of the many skilled makers out there. However, creating your own fursuit can prove to be an expensive venture, as the necessary parts—including foam, fur, fleece, and other fabrics and materials—add up quickly. And should you buy a custom-made fursuit, you're also looking at the cost of labour. Even pre-made suits, be they full (meaning a bodysuit along with a head, hands, feet and tail) or partial (often only including the head, tail and hands), can run anywhere from a couple hundred to a couple thousand dollars. But you don't need to have a suit of any kind in order to be a furry or to enjoy a fursona.

I definitely see my fursonas as extensions of myself, through which I can express myself more freely and creatively. My first fursona was Snowfall, the queer deer, whom I've always envisioned as a more bombastic and confident version of myself. They were pretty integral to my process of exploring my sexuality and gender identity in an open and authentic way in the early 2010s. They've had a few different looks since then, often reflecting changes that were simultaneously happening for me in terms of my body and identity. But I love that, like me, Snowfall is adorably chubby and fuzzy, with multiple facial piercings (in the same spaces that I have them), vibrant queer hair, long eyelashes and an overall playful confidence that exudes the love they have for themself.

Sadly, I don't yet have a Snowfall fursuit. However, I do have a partial fursuit (a head, tail and paws) for my other primary fursona: my sad boy opossum, Grey. He sits very close to my heart as he is representative of my lifelong experiences with depression, as well as being autistic and having ADHD. Grey embodies a lot of emotion, and a lot of trauma, but also growth, hope, passion, creativity and endurance. He's my moody guy, but he's also strong and I feel particularly comfortable and affirmed when I'm wearing him.

And of course, it can be sexy and affirming to incorporate your fursona, with or without part of a fursuit, into your look. While I do sometimes wear my fursuit of Grey for sexytimes with my partners, I also like to just play with small pet-play things. I might put on antlers that feel similar to how I envision they would for Snowfall, or I may wear more common pet-play items like cat ears, pup hoods or tails, whether or not I develop a full fursona around them. Again, there are no hard-and-fast rules.

Artwork by Dilutedghost depicting me (centre) alongside my fursonas, Snowfall (left) and Grey (right).

LEATHER, KINK AND FETISH WEAR

Of all the vibes we'll cover, this one can easily be the most sexually explicit. You don't have to go all out, of course. Leather and kink can be as subtle as you want it to be. In your casual or business clothing, you can incorporate aspects of your kinky side by using BDSM and fetish gear to bring a daring edge to any outfit. But many people love to go fucking all out!

Leather, for many people, serves as a second skin of sorts. Not only does it literally go over your skin, but it also provides a layer of protection that encourages many to let go of their inhibitions. Folks who wear leather tend to express feeling braver, more capable and freer to be themselves in any and all spaces they inhabit. Wearing gear under work clothes, or wearing accessories like cuffs or a collar while out at a social event, can be all it takes to bring out a little excitement. Leather can also help you access characteristics and strengths that you might normally reserve for more intimate settings, but that may prove to be uplifting in your day-to-day life as well.

Dominants may find that wearing leather or fetish gear in any scenario helps them feel more powerful and confident. Putting on their favourite pair of boots may help them navigate socializing at a party that would otherwise be too overwhelming to even attend, while wearing a chest harness under a dress shirt to a work presentation heightens their communication and delivery in a way that no other self-affirming charm or ritual could. Just as Clark Kent becomes Superman when he dons his cape, many folks feel like they transform into new people in leather and fetish wear.

In terms of intimacy and sexual spaces, leather and fetish wear can signify an interest in rougher and more experimental sex and pleasure. And kink can lead to powerful experiences: a Dominatrix transforms into another version of herself as her sub finishes lacing up her knee-high leather boots, the heel of which rests on their thigh; the sub finally lets go of all their fear and shame to allow themself true sexual freedom the instant that their Dominatrix fastens a ball gag in their mouth.

By choosing what pieces to use and wear in the various circumstances of your life, you can curate your look and your sex life into one all-encompassing, transgressive and empowering expression.

Left, **Unkle Daddy;** *right*, **K Rivers and Honey G.**

LUMBERSEXUALS

While not strictly a queer style, the lumberjack look hints at beautiful homoeroticism within even the straightest of contexts. Similar to butch queers, lumbersexuals also tend to see their vibe as more than a style and more of an identity. For a lot of masc trans and nonbinary queers, a lumbersexual aesthetic can be an empowering way of approaching rugged masculinity with a challenging playfulness. Historically, the lumberjack embodies a lot of traditional manliness. From brute strength to determined survivalism, lumberjacks are Men with a capital "M" who hunt, survive off the land, defend themselves against all manner of beasts, tame the wilds and, of course, chop down really fucking big trees with the raw power of their really fucking big arms.

That shit is sexy as heck, right!?

So, in a queer context, a lumbersexual takes those ultra-masculine tropes and completely recontextualizes them. Expressing yourself in this style sends the message that you too are strong, capable, rugged and formidable, yet also soft, loving, approachable and stylish. It says that you can be a badass even as you suck dick, or date cute trans queers, or enjoy cuddles and affection without any of that invalidating your manliness. Because that's the thing, your personal manliness is entirely what you make of it.

Plus, it's just a damn good look!

Lumbersexuals thrive in fitted plaid shirts (sometimes with a basic white T-shirt underneath), stylish suspenders, leather belts with nice buckles, and tuques, all of which is accentuated by beautifully styled hair and a nicely manicured beard or mustache. Seriously, as a queer with a beard myself, I appreciate folks who put the work into grooming, shaping and beautifying their facial hair, proudly incorporating it into their look, and I can think of no better example than the fabulous lumbersexual. Of course, you can still rock your rugged, outdoorsy, queer mountain-man self while stubbly or clean shaven.

At first glance, it might be easy to confuse lumbersexuals with hipsters. However, whereas the latter leans heavily into mixing with urban styles, the former is deeply rooted in rural aesthetics. It's about both embracing and subverting woodsman manliness, all in one gloriously plaid-infused go.

COTTAGECORE LESBIAN

This vibe has taken off in queer lesbian spaces online since 2020. I love it because it's kind of the natural counterpart to the lumbersexual. Once again, this aesthetic is about more than just the style, as it centres a desire to reject the overwhelming nature of city life. In an *Advocate* article entitled "What Is a Cottagecore Lesbian?" writer Christine Linnell explains, "Much of the cottagecore movement is actually a response to people being dissatisfied with their hectic, crowded lives in cities or suburbs, and the feelings of burnout that come with it."[12]

So, not only is cottagecore a look, but it's also a way of living, including home decor. Many cottagecore lesbians fill their apartments with potted plants, porcelain teacups, old-fashioned furniture and natural lighting, and spend

---

12 Christine Linnell, "What Is a Cottagecore Lesbian?"
The Advocate, July 10, 2020. https://www.advocate.com/women/2020/7/10/what-cottagecore-lesbian.

their free time enjoying comfort hobbies like crafts, baking, knitting, painting and making pottery.

In terms of style, cottagecore clothing options include a lot of linen dresses, sun hats, knitted sweaters, floral patterns, light colours, lace collars, summer dresses, lace-up brown leather boots, Mary Jane shoes, floral high-ankle canvas shoes, jean overalls, white frilly socks, and so on and so forth. It's a serious vibe, and I dig how, like lumbersexuals with rugged mountain manliness, cottagecore lesbians take the idea of the traditional farm wife and make it real freakin' gay!

PREPPY GAY

Oh, the preppy gay! It's like if middle-class '80s suburban boys all just took a collective deep breath and realized it's OK that they were dressing flagrantly queer and it's OK to want to kiss your bros.

I don't see the preppy homosexual or "sweater queen" look as much nowadays, but it's still there in a lot of theatre culture, on some college campuses, at the odd suburban backyard barbecue, and especially in more professional, business-y spaces. The preppy gay is most likely to appear on a golf course with their coworkers, or poolside at the country club, or at family functions at fancy restaurants, or during rehearsals for a community theatre production.

Prep relies a lot on high-society fashion, including yacht-club casual wear, college frat-boy attire and expensive private school uniforms, with its own degree of individuality in styling. But for trans and nonbinary queers, that individuality comes out even more, as they bring an air of insolence and sardonicism into the look. The preppy gay is sassy as fuck. They're not so much flaunting class and wealth—they're accessorizing with it, flamboyantly rocking it and, in some cases, even parodying it. Look, a preppy gay just knows they look good!

TWINKS

I love how consistent twinks have been throughout the decades. They've always had a vibe, a look, and in so many ways, it's the same now as it's ever been. Crop tops, booty shorts (the brighter the better), tight and revealing jean shorts, pastel polo shirts, tank tops, mesh tops, and all things queer, explicit and flirty. Twinks are proud of how cute and desirable they are. Most are either happily being flaunted by, and flaunting themselves for, their daddies, or they're actively in search of one. Often seen under the care of a bear, twinks sport tight graphic T-shirts with slogans like "Oh hi, Daddy," "power bottom" or "boy toy."

Historically speaking, twinks have always been depicted as young, slim, and free of facial or body hair. They exemplify masculine boyhood, focusing heavily on playfulness, curiosity, brattiness and beauty in their own right. A twink defies traditional gender roles by embracing traits, mannerisms and behaviours generally seen as feminine and incorporating them into queer, youthful masculinity. They are flamboyant and campy, and they approach everything, especially their own self-expression, with exuberance and a smidge of theatricality. They demand attention, praise and care because they are adorable and sexy and goddammit, they deserve it!

Nowadays, twinks can come in all shapes and sizes, sometimes even with more fluff. Some can also be buff and older, often referred to as muscle twinks. I'm also delighted to report that trans boys have made an enormous splash in the twink scene and are absolutely nailing it by bringing their own unique flavour of soft boi energy into the mix through a harder steer into androgyny and heightened sensuality.

Exploring twink style is not all about sexualizing yourself, though. Many twinks also have a good sense of casual and professional fashion. Outside of the campier, more flamboyant looks, you may also find a twink just hanging out in a jersey and athletic shorts, or khakis and a white T-shirt, or a plaid button-up and jeans, or even something a little punk, preppy or goth. I'm also particularly fond of trans guy twinks who often just rock a binder with some unfastened overalls or pants and an open dress shirt. It's just a really good look! For me, explicit trans and nonbinary queer expressions from folks using trans-affirming clothing will never outstay their welcome.

THE WITCHY GOTH

Goth is a great vibe all on its own, but since we're looking specifically at trans and nonbinary queer takes on various aesthetics, what fits even better than the basics is the Witchy Goth. A noticeable percentage of trans girls love this style and rock it so damn hard.

Powerful, dark, dramatic and magical, this look pulls inspiration from all things witchcraft and Wiccan. Some people may lean more into worldly paganism, while others draw from a fairy-tale interpretation, both of which are awesome and empowering. Witchy goth looks include a surprising range of vibes for self-expression beyond what you may find in the darker, bleaker goth styles. Witchy goth can still go dark, but it also includes a dusty and earthy palette, as nature, the earth and symbology around the cycle of life and death are very important to some people who love this look. And for a romanticized approach to it all, you can incorporate asymmetrical, tattered and ravaged fabrics with murky colours that bring in an air of mysticism.

Of course, we can't ignore how this whole scene quite clearly challenges the entire institution of organized religion and traditional god-fearing belief structures. There's nothing Christian about witchy goths who, if spirituality does play into their aesthetic, choose to explore and express that entirely on their own terms. Their power stems from the potions, spells, incantations and rituals they've crafted to uplift themselves, bolster their self-perception and radically reshape their world.

It's not surprising to me that all of this re-imagining makes the whole vibe an enormous draw for trans femmes and enby babes. I mean, isn't that all just the fucking gayest?

Goddexx Puti, Goddexx Inti, and La Muxer Diosa star in *Crash Pad Series* "Episode 342."

MODERN BEARS AND THE DREAM DADDY

Several of the previously discussed styles can play into this look, because being a bear is more of an identity than it is any singular look. Bear identity is about embracing your masculine self—body hair, weight, age and all—and then incorporating it into any other style you choose. You'll see leather bears, lumber bears, preppy bears, butch bears, pup-play bears, camp bears and more. They're all out there, and they're all amazing!

The biggest aspect I've noticed in bear culture is body acceptance and positivity, especially for larger masc folks. A lot of queer bears tend to be hairy, chubby, or buff and broad-shouldered. Some bears are Dominants and embody serious Daddy energy, while others are soft, affectionate, cuddly and may prefer being topped. In more social settings, bears' style prioritizes an unabashed look that complements their size, while in more intimate settings, they don't shy away from letting their belly hang, their fluffiness shine and their personality glow. Some of my absolute favourite sexy bear looks range from explicit—like wearing nothing but a leather harness and jockstrap—to casual—like an unbuttoned, open plaid shirt, loosened belt and fitted slacks. Hells yeah!

Meanwhile, the dream Daddy delightfully centres the queerification of the suburban husband or father look that's typically associated with cishet family men. Like with bears, a Daddy, and more specifically a dream Daddy, can encompass a range of masculine gender expressions, from a barbecue-dad look (maybe some comfy sweats and a tank top) to a more masculine homemaker vibe, complete with an apron and matching oven mitts. The important bit is that whatever the style, it comes in brighter colours, more flamboyant patterns and tighter fits because, mmm! Yes, Daddy!

Dick Hamby and Vic Novio star in
***Crash Pad Series* "Episode 367."**

This concludes our tour of selected queer and trans looks you might find inspiring. You'll find many more as you start exploring. Look around, see what grabs your interest, and have fun trying things on for size!

BODILY ALTERATIONS

Beyond styles of dress, you might also choose to explore other ways of changing your look, whether temporary or permanent. Options can include anything from haircuts to plastic surgery, but I'm going to highlight two major areas of note here.

THE EXPRESSIVE POWER OF MAKEUP

Makeup isn't something that I typically apply to myself because I already struggle a lot with choosing affirming things to wear, and I mostly just want to get ready as quickly as possible. Lucky for me, my hubby Fenric is a master at cosmetics and he loves sitting me down, putting some music on and making me pretty. While I don't think I'd have the patience to do it myself, when Fen applies lipstick, eyeshadow and eyeliner to me, it feels deeply intimate. Not to mention that I look totally stunning and queer as hell when he's done!

Despite my struggles with doing it myself, for me, makeup tends to induce a strong gender euphoria, or more specifically a queer euphoria. It helps that I have long, gorgeous natural lashes. Applying mascara to them accentuates how stunning my eyes are and adds femininity to my face in a way that makes me feel genuinely gorgeous. The fact that I also have a beard at practically all times also lets me explore and express my gender nonconformity and fluidity in a really visible way, which I enjoy a lot.

One of my favourite trans sex bloggers, Quenby Harley, has always been very inspirational to me when it comes to the use of makeup in their expression. While I personally have more of an affinity for cosmetics focused on my eyes and lashes, they're all about the lipstick. "It can be quick and easy to do, yet still make a big difference in how I feel. By drawing focus to the bold colours on my lips, I shift it away from parts of my face I feel less comfortable with on that day and exert a degree of power over how I look," Harley explained in their "Trans Joy" blog series,[13] which explores how beautiful and fulfilling existing as a trans person can be, despite how negative the world is toward gender nonconformity. "The choice of colour can denote the intention and emotion I want to embody on that day. Red for seductive sensuality, pale blue for ethereal beauty and vulnerability. Most commonly I wear purple, for when I want the ferocious courage that characterizes Pride....For me lipstick evokes emotion, I feel powerful and beautiful when I wear it and applying it is a way to claim control over how I present to the world. And that is a joyous feeling."[14]

Not to mention that leaving lipstick kisses on somebody is sexy as fuck! That feeling of claiming control over how you express yourself to the world can be empowering. More often than not, we have no control over how cishet society sees and treats us based on our appearance, so feeling like you can at least present yourself in a way that makes you feel good, despite what any ignorant onlooker might think, can make a pretty big difference when navigating this world as a trans queer.

TATTOOS AND PIERCINGS

Regardless of what style or identity you gravitate toward in expressing yourself, your gender and/or your sexuality,

---

13 Quenby Harley, "Introducing: Trans Joy," *Quenby Creatives*, November 26, 2019. https://quenbycreatives.com/2019/11/26/introducing-trans-joy/.

14 Harley, "Trans Joy: Lipstick," *Quenby Creatives*, February 25, 2020. https://quenbycreatives.com/2020/02/25/trans-joy-lipstick/.

tattoos and piercings can add so much. Some of my most gender-euphoric experiences as a trans queer in recent years have come from my piercings. In early 2023, when I got the bridge of my nose pierced as a belated holiday present from my husband Fenric, I told him that it felt like it should have always been there. Leaving that appointment, I felt incredible, like my queerness was infinitely more affirmed and I looked more like how I perceived myself internally.

I felt similarly with each of my other facial piercings, especially my snakebites. And someday I hope to have a bunch of tattoos, too! They can be a tremendous source of self-expression and empowerment, regardless of where you get them on your body, whether they're in full colour or black and white, whether there's just one or they're all over your body. Tats are fucking hot!

You also don't need to actually get pierced or get a real tattoo in order to enjoy their benefits. Many accessory stores also carry faux piercings you can attach for the aesthetic, and you can also experiment with cool and realistic-looking temporary tattoos. Both options let you try things out without committing to the long-term alteration.

MANAGING YOUR EXPECTATIONS AROUND CONNECTIONS

So now you've got some idea of how to "be" sexy in terms of physical expression, you've gotten your look together a little more, found a vibe that you're into, and you're ready to get all dressed up and head out to the club, or bar, or into the bedroom. Is that where you'll start to actually *feel* sexy?

Ideally, yes! When you're looking hot, wearing the things that fit right and make you feel good, then hopefully you'll be feeling hot too. However, a big part of feeling sexy comes from a combination of how people express their attraction to you, and how you see yourself in that context.

So it's important to realize that just dressing in a sexy and complimentary way, while making you feel attractive, might not lead to the feelings you're hoping for if your overarching goal is predominantly to attract somebody else as a partner, lover or casual fling. Feeling attractive in that context also requires that another person show genuine interest, desires, or arousal in you as well, which of course in actuality isn't something we can "make" happen because we can't control others. (More about all this in the following chapters.)

What we can control, at least to some degree, is how we respond to these situations, and how we continue to perceive ourselves. While we can do things to improve our odds of finding connections and experiences that uplift and empower us, it remains supremely important to continue centring your own pleasure, happiness and fulfillment in these pursuits.

CHAPTER 7

DATING, FLIRTING AND FINDING COMMUNITY

Content Note: this chapter discusses transphobic and queerphobic violence that may be upsetting and triggering. Please take care in reading the section on "trans disclosure" in particular.

Where do you meet people who are safe and excited about forming connections with trans queers? How do you find other trans queers to date and explore with? How do you find connections with others who won't misgender you or touch you in ways that make you feel dysphoric? What do you do about all of the transphobia and queerphobia on dating and hookup apps? And if a nonsexual community is what you need, how do you go about finding it?

These are just some of the factors you may consider while navigating social and interpersonal spaces in general, to say nothing of spaces where you might forge romantic or sexual connections. It's tough enough for most people to find partners and lovers; for trans queers, it can be even tougher. We've all heard the horror stories of trans women being hurt or killed by men who felt threatened by them being trans. Trans people face some very real threats of severe violence when dating and seeking intimate bonds, and this possibility can be terrifying to think about.

Just take a look at the "LGBTQ+ panic" defense, also known as the "gay/trans panic" defense—an actual legal defense that has historically been used to justify assaulting or murdering queer and trans people because their identity was somehow a threat to the culprit. It's happened enough to be a well-documented tactic. And although this defense has been banned in many US states, it's still allowed in many others (more on this shortly). As well, a great deal of disturbing discourse still emerges from people who are more upset about the prospect of having sex with trans people than they are about trans people being murdered. Such people think the solution is for trans people to out themselves before every interaction they have with others—clearly not a fair or reasonable ask.

However, I assure you that you can find the connections you desire in safer ways, and you can take steps to protect yourself in those exchanges. In this chapter, we'll look at how to navigate dating apps, find safe partners and lovers, determine what you need and want in your relationships, express your personal boundaries, and find spaces where you can be yourself while forging the bonds that you desire.

WHERE TO FIND COMMUNITY AND TOGETHERNESS

Aside from finding your sexy and connecting with your sexual self, you may want to become more involved in trans queer social spaces. The easiest way to do so is to search for and reach out to your local Pride or LGBTQIA+ organizations. Many are run by and for trans queer communities, and some even have their own offices and community spaces. Depending on where you live and what's been established there, you may be able to find support groups, coffee meetups, educational resources, drop-in social spaces, poetry and art nights, presentations and workshops, rallies, flag-raisings, drag shows, and so much more.

And never forget: if you don't find what you need, you have the agency to build something new! If you live in a small town, consider contacting trans queer groups in nearby cities and letting them know that you want to make something local. Many would be more than willing to help, and members may even be willing to travel out to your town to be social and help you get set up.

You can also make online spaces such as Discord servers, Telegram chat channels or private Facebook groups, which others can join. Just be sure to develop a robust set of rules and community standards to deal with potential bad behaviour or conflicts. Or if you'd rather find an already-established space, then use the built-in search function on your social media platforms to see what's out there. Just type in your city's name, plus words such as "Pride,"

"LGBTQ," "trans" or "queer" in combination with "support," "group," "events" and other similar queries.

A word of warning: some spaces may seem trans queer–friendly at first, but eventually reveal themselves to be otherwise. In the wake of pushback against transgender folks, a handful of LGBTQ+ spaces and groups have decided that rather than support gender-diverse individuals, they'd instead splinter off and narrow their focus. Many of these organizations label themselves as being LG-only (for lesbians and gays) or LGB (which are inclusive of bisexual people, but not trans folks), and they tend to actively avoid the word "queer," as well as anyone who identifies as such. While not all of these groups are bigoted or harmful, many of their members express dissatisfaction with trans people, who they feel are bad for homosexual identities, and these groups often associate directly with and support anti-trans advocates.

"Gender critical" spaces are also harmful and best avoided. Members of gender-critical groups often claim not to be transphobic, yet these spaces focus on undermining gender-nonconforming identities, describing trans identities as nothing but forms of sexual fetishism, and trying to convince any trans folks who wander by that they're not actually trans and shouldn't want to be. I recommend keeping your distance from these areas of the internet and blocking gender-critical people and groups from your feeds to avoid incendiary transphobic comments and conversations.

But despite these very real concerns, don't be afraid out there. Explore and meet more trans queers, either as friends or more! Arguably the best way to find your sexy and feel more comfortable in your body and with your expression as a trans queer person is by seeing how other trans queer people are doing it. So get out to Pride if you can, socialize at those coffee meetups, check out those kinky events, and then chat, mingle and observe as best you can. It takes some doing, but you'll find your people soon enough.

TRANS "DISCLOSURE": WHAT IT IS AND WHY YOU DON'T HAVE TO DO IT

Many people have heated opinions on whether or not trans people need to disclose that they are trans to potential dates. Mostly it's cis people who freak out about this conversation, and transphobia and queerphobia are at the crux of these "debates." When you get through the "why" of it all, most people who want trans people to disclose their identities in their profiles, or immediately after matching, feel this way because they just don't want to date trans people. They've heard and bought into myths and fallacies about us, or they're scared of what their family, friends or peers may think about them if they were to date one of us. Rather than deal with those issues, they want us to warn them about our existence.

It's bullshit. It all feeds into the major issue of fear around trans bodies, and the violence that can sometimes be perpetrated based on that fear. Every year, numerous trans queer people, especially trans women of colour, are killed while attempting to date and daring to merely exist.

It is not trans people's responsibility to hide who they are in order to avoid becoming victims of transphobic violence.

Our legal and educational systems are letting us down by not protecting us and by not including education around trans and queer identities and bodies. In many parts of North America, schools barely have comprehensive sex ed as it is, and they certainly don't have any that acknowledges the existence of trans queers—though some districts have recently begun including sexual orientation and gender identity in the curriculum.

Meanwhile, the LGBTQ+ panic defense mentioned earlier in this chapter is still legal in all but 19 US states as of December 2023, according to the LGBTQ+ Bar, an association of legal professionals working with LGBTQ+ legal organizations. The LGBTQ+ Bar describes this defense as "a legal strategy that asks a jury to find that a victim's sexual orientation or gender identity/expression is to blame for a defendant's violent reaction, including murder."[15]

In Canada, while it's not very common, the LGBTQ+ panic defense has been used and is still technically allowed in any province. In a 2021 article for *In Magazine* called "Queer Crime: The Gay/Trans Panic Defense Is Still a Thing," Courtney Hardwick points out that the defense is allowed under the Criminal Code of Canada's definition of provocation, which is described as "a wrongful act or insult that is of such a nature as to be sufficient to deprive an ordinary person of the power of self-control." The purpose of the defense is to help the alleged perpetrator avoid first-degree murder convictions not by denying guilt, but by justifying it, Hardwick explains. If the defense team can prove there

---

15 The LGBTQ+ Bar, "LGBTQ+ 'Panic' Defense." https://lgbtqbar.org/programs/advocacy/gay-trans-panic-defense/.

was provocation, a murder charge may be reduced to a much less serious sentence of manslaughter. "Sometimes the defense uses past trauma to paint a story of PTSD that could lead to uncontrollable violence but proving a defendant's state of mind (or mens rea), at the time of the crime, is difficult," writes Hardwick. "Therefore, a gay/trans panic defense is basically asking a jury to look at a crime through a homophobic lens that considers flirting while gay or trans a justification for murder."[16]

Despite the existence of the gay/trans panic defense, and the possible ramifications of revealing more about your gender identity and details of your body, I feel that you absolutely do not need to reveal that you're trans to anyone until you feel safe and comfortable enough with them to do so. Choosing not to disclose can protect you from the possibility of negative, adverse or violent reactions.

That being said, if you are a trans queer person hoping to connect with other trans queer people, I strongly suggest you make your sexuality and gender identity very clear—not because you have to, but because that's what many other trans queers will be looking for. They're likely searching for folks like themselves, with whom they'll feel safe, comfortable and affirmed. Some people use the indicator "t4t" on their profiles, which means they are a trans person interested in other trans people. Doing the same will help you connect with like-minded trans and nonbinary queers a lot more easily.

---

16 Courtney Hardwick, "Queer Crime: The Gay/Trans Panic Defense Is Still a Thing," *In Magazine*, February 24, 2021. https://inmagazine. ca/2021/02/queer-crime-the-gay-trans-panic-defence-is-still-a-thing/.

YOUR NEEDS, WANTS AND NONNEGOTIABLES WHILE SEEKING SOCIAL AND INTIMATE CONNECTIONS

In "Chapter 16: Sexuality" of the second edition of *Trans Bodies, Trans Selves*, published by Oxford University Press, I wrote:

> *Needs are things we absolutely require in our relationships either emotionally, romantically, affectionately, or sexually. For some of us, this might mean strong communication, honesty, not being abused, or living in a certain geographic region. Needs may also revolve around sexual require- ments—including "hard no's" on specific sex acts, certain words, or types of touch that we may find traumatic or invalidating. One way to determine our needs is to ask ourselves what we require from our relationships—sexual or otherwise—to feel most comfortable, supported, encouraged, and fulfilled.*

What I didn't get to explore much was how needs translate in practical and personal terms. For example, it is supremely important that I feel queer, and that the people I'm close to don't treat me as if I were a cisgender man. I need all of my partners, lovers, dates and even friends to not only acknowledge that my identity exists and is important to me, but also to work with me in building an environment in which queerness and gender diversity are consistently valued and valorized.

By this, I mean that my relationships cannot be hidden or otherwise closeted, and instead need to be celebrated and openly enjoyed. It means that my partners and I should always have the freedom to express our affection with one another in public or around family and friends, and that at no time is anyone expected to tone themselves down in terms of their self-expression. I dress very queer. I wear dresses, skirts and other femme-coded clothing mixed with a range of gender-neutral and masc-coded items. I also have lots of body hair, a thick beard and long curly hair. I talk with a very soft voice that I've been told sounds incredibly gay, and I love that. At times in my life, various people have been embarrassed about these traits of mine, and I've tried to force myself to be what they wanted me to be. They pressured and guilted me into shaving, dressing differently in public or around their family, and even practicing speaking with a different voice. All of those choices put me in negative emotional states where I felt unsafe and bad about being myself, which in turn led to deep depression and overwhelming dysphoria. Never again! I now strive for the exact opposite of those past experiences. This priority is so crucial in my life that I am entirely incapable of feeling sexy, or even safe, if this need is not met.

I've also come to learn that I also need my partners and lovers to identify as trans queer. This need arises from a long history of struggles with having cisgender partners who were not able to grasp the nuances of having trans partners, and while I acknowledge that people who are not familiar with trans bodies need to be treated with a degree of patience and given education, I also know that I am not obliged to constantly put myself in the role of a teacher or mentor in my intimate relationships. I deserve to have fulfilling and enriching bonds that don't require being a "trans 101" experience for the other person.

The needs I've described so far are *nonnegotiables* for me. A nonnegotiable need is significantly more entrenched than any other kind, and not meeting it is often a deal-breaker. A nonnegotiable should not be formed lightly. In keeping with what I've already shared, one of my absolute biggest nonnegotiables is that I require that my relationships not be cisnormative or heteronormative in any way, and that they not contain any degree of traditional gender roles or expectations, and that my body, my identity and the words I use to describe both not be up for debate. If I feel that someone is invalidating my identity, or that our interactions don't feel affirming or empowering in regard to my queerness, then that's not a bond I am willing to continue pursuing.

The thing about needs, though, is that while some can be very firm, such as the ones I just mentioned, others have at least a little breathing room for adaptation as required. Take yet another of my needs: I need to not be put back into a closet of any kind, and I require my relationships to be open and visible in their queerness so that I may enjoy, celebrate and appreciate them fully. But as important as those requirements are for me, they do come with the caveat that I am willing to be partially closeted in specific circumstances, and for a finite amount of time. For example, if I were getting involved with somebody who needed a little bit of time to work themself up to telling their family that they were polyamorous, but who was actively working on a plan and would execute it in the near future, then I wouldn't mind being discreet around their family until they were ready to disclose.

Wants are far more malleable. In *Trans Bodies, Trans Selves*, I wrote:

> *Wants are things we could potentially go without in a relationship or may be subject to compromise. A want might look like going on more dates, receiving certain types of pleasure (such as oral sex), or experiencing certain types of play (such as public sex or watersports, where one partner urinates on another). If we're okay with possibly not getting something, it isn't a need. While having our wants met would certainly be wonderful, we could accept it if our partner(s), lover(s), or play friends(s) didn't want those same things.*

Unlike needs, wants are a lot more flexible. Take, for example, this very ironic fact about me, especially when considering what this book is all about: while I truly want to feel sexy, I don't necessarily have to feel sexy in order to be content in my relationships or to feel fulfilled in my intimate connections. Feeling sexy is not only subjective, but has often been difficult for me, especially since I struggle a lot with depression, anxiety, PTSD and insecurities from personal trauma. And that's all on top of the social and cultural stuff that makes me feel like as a fat, hairy trans queer in my late thirties, I'm not widely considered a particularly attractive individual (which is hot garbage and incorrect, of course). If I absolutely needed to feel sexy in order to explore sexual intimacy or have meaningful emotional connections, then I frankly wouldn't be sexually active, because it's an ongoing struggle for me. Feeling sexy is more of a want—it's something I'd very much like, but it isn't essential to my ability to connect with others or have the experiences I desire.

Whatever your needs and wants, it's important to understand which ones are essential to your safety and wellness, and which ones you are willing to compromise on or let go of entirely for the connections that otherwise feel right for you. Because there is no perfect match out there. No one person is ever going to be everything you've ever wanted—as we're about to explore.

HAVING REASONABLE EXPECTATIONS WHEN MAKING, OR MISSING, CONNECTIONS

Here's the thing about your needs, wants and nonnegotiables: they're meant to guide you, but not to control or influence other people's opinions or behaviours. If somebody isn't meeting your needs, if a bond isn't giving you what you want, it's important to express that to the other person. But it's also important to do so with an understanding that they may not be able to give you what you require or desire...and that's OK. Your partner, lover or friend isn't responsible for meeting all of your needs. That's an impossibly large amount of pressure and expectation to put onto any single person.

It's all about deciding what you can and can't live without, and considering those wants and needs in a realistic and compassionate way within the unique contexts of each of your connections. For example, maybe you're having a lot of frustrations with a particular friendship. If it's important to you to feel like you can count on your friends when you need support and to socialize together at least a few times a month, but they have a tendency to flake on plans or to not respond to your messages for days at a time, maybe you need to start reconsidering that connection. You don't have to entirely end the friendship, but you may want to express how you feel—without accusation—rather than just let your feelings sit and fester into bitterness. Maybe the convo will go great and you'll start seeing some changes that make you feel more connected to your friend. That would be great! But it might not go that way. Should they continue flaking, cancelling on your plans a lot and not responding to messages, it may be time for you to either reassess your expectations of that friendship or consider not investing in it as much as you'd like.

Not everyone has the same emotional availability, communication and friendship needs. That doesn't make them, or you, a bad person; it just means you're in a different place when it comes to the way you approach your connections and the needs and wants you've identified. Just remember that while you don't have to accept a friendship that isn't fulfilling, you also can't force somebody into being the friend you wish they would be. You can work on the friendship together with compassion and patience, or adjust your expectations of that bond so that it feels better to you, or choose to let it go. All are completely valid approaches.

These reconsiderations and reflections also may be important for more intimate desires and connections in your life. For example, if you're a kinky person and find yourself dating and falling in love with somebody who isn't, yet you feel an intense need to have those kinky desires fulfilled, you'll have a lot to consider. To start, it's worth opening a dialogue with this person about your needs, explaining their importance to you, and asking if there are any types of kinky activities they'd be open to doing with you, whether big or small, frequent or occasional. Maybe some spanking or even casual bondage every now and then would work for both of you. Keep in mind that if your needs and wants are more on the level of a 24/7 BDSM dynamic, that may be a more difficult desire for a non-kinky partner to fulfill. So, if you're looking for a hard Dom to top you as a dedicated submissive, you may want to put that out there immediately and treat it as a nonnegotiable.

But let's say you have had this discussion. You really like this person and are willing to let go of your more intense submissive wants, but they have expressed that kink is a hard limit for them, something they're not comfortable with, even a little bit. Now come the more difficult questions.

As a kinky and submissive person, can you remain in a long-term, committed, monogamous connection with somebody who is uncomfortable with and unwilling to explore kink with you? How substantial is your need for kink and submission when it comes to your sexual pleasure and fulfillment? Would you consider discussing the possibility of an open relationship with your non-kinky partner, wherein you can ethically engage with other people to meet your BDSM needs? And in the event that they are absolutely not comfortable with that, are you willing to accept that those needs will never be fulfilled while you're with your partner?

Notice how none of these questions involve any degree of forcing, or attempting to coerce or convince, your partner to do anything they are uncomfortable doing. That's because we simply cannot control others, and frankly we shouldn't even try to, as that can veer into manipulation, guilting, shaming and abuse. All we can control is ourselves. It's important to prepare yourself for the inevitability that not everybody you are interested in or attracted to is going to be interested in or attracted to you, or desire the same things as you.

NAVIGATING TRANSPHOBIA AND QUEERPHOBIA ON DATING SITES

Sadly, dating for trans queers can be pretty rough. Folks who use the big dating apps face an often tremendously transphobic user base rife with misgendering, invalidation and bizarre objectification. Several of my friends and peers have had their accounts locked and banned for "getting a lot of complaints" after they were reported repeatedly by transphobic users. This scenario is especially common for trans women on mainstream apps, where users can report people for being "fake" or "misleading." Transphobes often use these rules to argue that they felt somehow deceived by a trans woman, which is of course vile and blatantly bigoted. This issue has been widely reported for several years but nothing seems to have changed.

Spaces and apps used predominantly for fast hookups are widely cisnormative; most folks are seeking other cis people to get off with. That cisnormativity is present not only on more heterosexual-focused sites and apps, but also on many gay and lesbian ones, on which the majority of cis queer folks often don't seem to care about being considerate in their communication. They're just looking to fuck, or be fucked by, other cis queers. If you're not cis, you face an uphill battle the vast majority of the time. Based on my own experiences, and those of most of my partners and friends, trans people seeking relationships or sex on these sites tend to experience a lot of invasive questions, disheartening (and sometimes demeaning) rejections and offensive remarks. They are also frequently expected to do a lot of emotional labour by having politicized conversations about trans social-justice issues and listening to transphobic takes disguised as opinions. Other times, they are expected to accept and ignore misgendering or to justify the validity of their identity and argue for the basic respect of their pronouns.

Even the queer dating apps that are explicitly more inclusive in their marketing, gender identity options, and focus on bringing together a diverse range of trans and nonbinary queers aren't without their problems. They, too, can be difficult for trans users, who may find themselves facing transphobia on these platforms despite their progressive messaging and policies. Issues and divisions within the community out in the world tend to pour into those intimate spaces online and can create harmful environments even in those striving to be safe. Over my many, many years of dating trans and nonbinary queers, and talking with trans queer friends, I've heard all manner of horror stories—gross fetishization of transness, stalking behaviours, floods of messages from random users laughing at them and attacking their gender identity. I haven't found much affirmation in my own experiences as a nonbinary queer using dating apps. My pronouns are almost never acknowledged, and anytime I attempt to ask for them to be used, and ask that my identity be respected, I've been met with ridicule, invalidation, demeaning commentary on my "made-up gender" and a bunch of awful gender-essentialist takes on "biology."

That's not to say you can't find some positive experiences on the apps, of course; not all users are major dickbags. I have managed to meet some cool trans queer individuals on online dating sites, some of whom I've hooked up with or dated. They're just few and far between.

When possible, using local trans queer social spaces to try to meet people is likely a much better option. That strategy comes with its own hurdles and awkwardness, especially when considering accessibility concerns and safety precautions around COVID-19, and you need to be mindful of context by not trying to pick anyone up at, say, a support group. But I've had much better experiences meeting people and forging friendships that have the potential to become more by attending coffee meetups, LGBTQ+ social events, dances, poetry nights and more gatherings along those lines.

If you do want to give the more mainstream dating apps a go, I strongly recommend that you emotionally prepare yourself for some of the potential toxicity, frustration and hurt that you may experience. Additionally, don't shy away from unmatching, blocking and reporting if you find yourself being harassed, ridiculed or attacked about your gender identity or sexuality. And don't ignore the red flags and bad vibes! If somebody is making you uncomfortable about your gender or sexuality, or if they're saying borderline problematic things, vaguely complaining about "**wokeness**," or repeating any form of ignorant rhetoric about trans queers, run away. Don't minimize it, ignore it or excuse it. Trust your gut.

WHEN "PREFERENCES" ARE ACTUALLY BIGOTED

"No fats. No fems. No Asians." I could actually feel my jaw drop in shock the first time I ever read those words on a profile on a gay dating app. Surely that level of prejudice was just a one-off, right?

Wrong. Turns out it's incredibly common. I learned that a shocking number of people seem to think there's nothing inherently wrong or bigoted about outright writing off entire populations of people based on their race and ethnicity, disabilities, bodies and more. They often see these beliefs as "preferences," not reflections of who they are and what values and ideals they hold. Of course, that's far from the truth. Choosing to exclude certain groups of people from your dating pool reveals a great deal about the beliefs and assumptions you hold about those groups.

A preference is something like "I don't want any long-distance relationships because I find them too difficult emotionally," or "I am monogamous and would not feel comfortable dating somebody who is polyamorous or nonmonogamous." Hell, I'll even give you that wanting to date people who are thin and taller than you can be a preference...though I'd argue that it's incredibly superficial, discounts a lot of things that are not in anybody's control, and is a clear sign of some pretty major fatphobia and body-negativity issues.

I'm not going to pull any punches here. Refusing to date people based on things they cannot control, like the colour of their skin, or their disabilities, or their weight and height, is simply prejudiced. To say that you are not emotionally, romantically or sexually interested in all people belonging to a certain ethnic group—not just some, but all of them—is not a "preference." It's racism. To say that you wouldn't date anyone who is depressed, or autistic, or uses a mobility aid isn't a "preference." It's ableism. And to say that you wouldn't date a trans person, no matter what, isn't a "preference" either. It's transphobia.

A lot of these attempts to disguise prejudice goes on even in LGBTQ+ spaces, particularly among people who identify as lesbian or gay. Many people seem to think that it's not transphobic to refuse to date trans people because that's "just their sexuality." What that belief doesn't consider is that trans people aren't monolithic. Not feeling comfortable being sexually intimate with somebody who has a penis is one thing, but to use that as justification to discriminate against all trans women, and to reject them in an invalidating way based on your assumptions about their genitals, is not justifiable. Because trans women are not all the same. Some have penises, some don't; some are comfortable being sexual with them, some don't use them as part of sex at all. For example, somebody saying they are a lesbian and they refuse to date any trans women is also saying that they do not see trans women as women. And I'm sorry, but yes, that's transphobic.

A good test to consider whether a preference is based on prejudice is to ask yourself why. Why would you not want to date anyone with mobility struggles, or anyone belonging to a certain ethnic group? I'm willing to bet that the answer isn't one you'd want to say out loud because it sounds incredibly ableist or racist, no matter how you might try and phrase it.

If you don't want to date a certain demographic without doing any self-reflection to better understand what that may say about you and your ideals, that's fine. For their sake, I agree that you likely shouldn't date them, as getting involved with you would probably be harmful to them. But you don't have to say so. There is no reason whatsoever for you to put racist, ableist or transphobic caveats on your profile.

If somebody messages you and you're not interested in pursuing them based on some aspect of their identity, then don't pursue them. In fact, you don't even have to respond! You don't need to give them a reason. You don't need to tell a trans person that you're not interested in them because they are trans. Saying that is not kind. It's unnecessarily mean, because at best it makes them feel bad about themselves for something they cannot control.

There's no upside to showing your bigotry. So if you aren't into someone, just ignore them and move on.

HOW TO FLIRT WITH OTHER TRANS QUEERS

Quite possibly one of the biggest tropes about trans queers flirting is that we don't know when we're being flirted with, and we think that we suck at it. In reality, we actually flirt really well and just need to get better at reading one another and accepting that somebody else has an interest in us. My experience with trans queers is that they are all endearingly, amazingly, catastrophically, awkwardly, so friggin' cute and they don't even know it!

So often, people ask me how they can be less embarrassing and come off as more self-assured. And each time, I say the same thing: don't. Awkwardness in the trans queer dating scene is gold. Ask most other trans queers out there, and the vast majority will confirm it. Seriously, I stand by that claim!

Awkward, shy, clumsy, nerdy trans queers fumbling through conversation are hot, endearing and interesting, and always find themselves with great relationships and lots of equally adorable friends. So, if you're worried that you might be a bumbling mess, I'm here to tell you that you should embrace it and lean into that shit! Don't try to force yourself into being somebody you're not or trying to perform traditional cishet courtship behaviours. Those strategies rarely ever work in trans queer spaces.

If you regularly stumble all over your words, it's OK. Stumble on, friend! If you don't know how to dance and have often been told you look like one of those wacky, waving, inflatable-arm-flailing tube men outside of a car dealership, then hell yeah. Wag those limbs and shake those hips! We trans queers love a floundering cutie!

BEING HUMBLE AND SHOWING EMPATHY IN REJECTION

While it always stings when somebody turns you down, decides against a second date or ultimately finds that there's not enough meshing between you and starts to de-escalate things, try your best not to internalize every rejection. Believe me, I get it, and I know that's easier said than done, especially if you were feeling good about things, or were feeling sexy and confident in yourself before the person turned you down. Rejection, regardless of its intent, feels pretty damn personal. It might even feel insulting, invalidating or critical.

In actuality, if somebody isn't into you or your look, although that will certainly feel bad, it's not a reflection on you as an individual or on your overall attractiveness. It's merely a reflection of the other individual's desires and what appeals to them personally. Not matching what they're looking for is just that: a mismatch. And you're much better off finding somebody who goes absolutely wild over you instead.

Of course, you're allowed to feel bad when you experience rejection. In fact, I strongly recommend you allow yourself to feel everything you need to. Sad, angry, hurt, bitter, frustrated, jealous, insecure, scared—it's all valid stuff. I've felt it all too!

Once upon a time, I was flirting with this cute queer guy at a sex party. Things seemed cool, and it felt like we clicked personality-wise, so I messaged him afterward. But he replied and told me that while he enjoyed talking to me, he couldn't see himself with another dude. It wasn't my fault, but, and

I quote, "I have a really hard time with male bodies." This comment hurt me on multiple levels because not only does rejection suck in general, but I'm also a nonbinary queer. This guy, who knew I was nonbinary and used they/them pronouns, went out of his way to misgender me and tell me that it came down to the fact that he could not see me as anything but another man. To him, I had what he perceived to be a cis male body, and therefore he didn't want to be intimate with me in any way.

Now, all of that may have been true, and he had every right to not enter into any sort of intimate bond with me. However, he didn't need to tell me any of the other crap. He very well could have just said, "I'm sorry, but I'm not interested in something like that right now." It wasn't necessary to give an explanation why, let alone one that was transphobic and deeply hurtful. Hearing somebody tell me that it's nothing personal, but my "male" body betrays and undermines me as a nonbinary person and makes me undesirable—that is a lot to take in. It made me feel like complete garbage, and I made sure to tell him that in the hope that he wouldn't do it to any other trans folks. In fact, rejecting anybody because of their body doesn't help. It just hurts. There are absolutely kinder ways to let somebody down that don't centre on criticizing their looks or identity.

After that harsh rejection, which felt so very cruel, I let myself feel all of the emotion I needed to (which in this case was mainly seething anger) and reminded myself that it wasn't actually about me. It was about him. What he was projecting on me wasn't a reflection of who I was. Rather, it spoke more to his lack of knowledge about trans queer people, his limited understanding of gender and bodies, and his inconsiderate communication around navigating rejection. In the end, his perceptions about me were wrong, and I refused to get down on myself about them any further.

If you too are turned down for your body, gender or anything else outside of your control, know that it is not a reflection of your worth or desirability as a person—it's an indication of the other person's perceptions. Their perceptions do not define you, and you are not lesser for not being what they expected or hoped for. Keep rocking your awesome self and you'll find people who genuinely see, value and want you!

CHAPTER 8
TRANS QUEER–AFFIRMING SEX: WHAT IT IS AND HOW TO HAVE IT

~~~~~~

Content Note: this chapter contains sexually explicit descriptions and sexually suggestive images used to help illustrate the topics and acts being discussed.

~~~~~~

Affirming yourself as a trans queer, seeing yourself as a sexual being who is worthy of fulfillment and is desirable to others, is clearly a lot of work. Once you've done some of that work, it's also worth considering what affirming relationships and sex may look like for you, if you desire those things. But knowing what to look for is pretty tough when our culture doesn't tend to depict sexuality in empowering ways. Especially when it comes to positive sexual expression for trans queers!

But all is not lost. Now more than ever before, plenty of self-help books, blogs, websites, forums and content creators on various social media platforms focus on the needs of LGBTQ+ people. Also, while porn is not an ideal source of affirmation, due to how cisnormative and heteronormative it often is, some genuinely amazing adult content does exist that centres pleasure for trans queer people. A lot of us creatives have made enormous strides in generating trans queer–affirming, sex- and body-positive erotica, pornography, photography, art and more, which we do our best to put out there for as many people as possible to find. These voices and resources can prove to be immensely informative tools for your personal growth.

In this chapter, I'll share with you what trans queer–affirming sex looks like for me, how I define it, how diverse and creative it can be, and how to figure out whether you're in trans- and queer-affirming relationships. As well, I'll give you some ideas about where you can find adult content to aid in your own exploration.

If exploration is a strictly solo venture for you, that's valid too! In that case, I do hope you'll continue reading this chapter, because I strongly feel that much of what's said is still applicable. Especially if part of your goal is to connect more with your intimate or sexual self and to explore what brings you pleasure on your own. Your relationship with yourself, and the pleasure you give yourself, can also be trans queer–affirming!

WHY QUEER-AFFIRMING SEX AND PLEASURE ARE SO IMPORTANT TO ME

Up until just the last few years, sex has generally been a stressful and sometimes even invalidating experience for me. Overall, I felt like I wasn't able to understand or satisfy my own needs and wants, and by extension I also wasn't the lover that former partners expected me to be. Another major struggle was that many of my exes, especially those who were cisgender, did their best at exploring intimacy with a trans queer, but gender roles and expectations consistently crept into the bedroom in overwhelming ways. More often than not, I felt like I was being treated as a man typically would, and sex often felt very heteronormative in the sense that it was always assumed I'd be the one to initiate things, take charge and then have penetrative sex. Which was like, fine...but left me wanting something more.

I never knew exactly what to say, though, because I could never quite understand what was missing. All I knew was that, yeah, I was having orgasms, but I often felt empty afterward. In hindsight, a big problem for me was that sex didn't feel queer-affirming to me. It felt exactly like it did before I came out, like I was "the man with the penis" and as such, I had to be the assertive top who penetrated my partners.

Frustratingly, this issue persisted even with some trans queer partners and lovers. Almost all of them were bottoms who expected me to top them, to always be in control, confident and firm, to make them feel submissive and dominated, to be their sexual caregiver, and to get and maintain an erection to perform penetrative sex for long periods of time. So much was wrapped up in me "fucking" them "good and hard" that it eventually became a huge source of anxiety for me. If I couldn't do that, if I couldn't get an erection or if I didn't ejaculate or top them "right," then it was a problem. They'd be disappointed, sometimes even outright upset, and there'd be all this pressure. It's not that I dislike penetrative sex or topping, per se; I'm not even opposed to topping and domming somebody frequently. But after a while, it started to feel like because I had a beard and a dick, topping was just expected of me by default.

I didn't like being pushed into that role right off the bat. There just wasn't any room for me to explore myself in any other way than in the ways that others expected of me, and eventually the weight of those expectations eroded my confidence and skyrocketed my anxiety so much that I started to avoid sex entirely. When I did try to have sex with any of my partners, I'd struggle to get or maintain an erection, I wouldn't orgasm or ejaculate, and I'd want to get through it as quickly as possible while internally spiraling with feelings of immense inadequacy.

HOW I DEFINE QUEER-AFFIRMING SEX

From all of those experiences, I realized that while it is OK to have specific wants and desires for sexual intimacy and pleasure with your partners, it's not OK to try to push those wants and desires onto somebody else and pressure, guilt or shame them for not meeting your expectations. I decided I was no longer going to constantly compromise my own safety, pleasure and happiness in order to satisfy my partners.

Nowadays, for sex to be truly safe and affirming, in my eyes, it needs to:

1. Prioritize and ensure the emotional and physical safety of all involved
2. Have honest and considerate communication around needs, wants and boundaries. (As an autistic person with ADHD and high anxiety, I also immensely value direct and concise communication around these

things. While more detail is nice, I can have a hard time following important conversations if they go on for a long period of time and include a lot of side thoughts, backtracking or excess information.)

3. Have reasonable expectations that don't put anyone in potentially uncomfortable or invalidating positions

4. Have all participants seek and confirm continuous and enthusiastic consent with one another

5. Be free of pressure, guilt, manipulation, abuse and shame.

In addition, I especially value sex that is explicitly trans queer affirming! I want to feel like I am being truly seen for who I am, and that I'm not being invalidated in some weird cisnormative or heteronormative way. While this desire lines up with everything in my list above, it also includes some specific trans queer–related components. For me, sex is queer affirming when it fits these parameters:

1. Actively challenges, bends or rejects traditional, cisnormative and heteronormative roles and expectations around sexual pleasure

2. Is explicitly inclusive of trans and gender-diverse individuals, and is considerate of each partner's or lover's body, ability and mobility

3. Is open-minded, exciting, playful and fun in nature

4. Has a broad and diverse definition of sex and sexual pleasure that allows for a wide range of self-expression, varied activity, fulfilling experiences and shame-free kinky goodness.

If some of my criteria resonate for you as well, that's awesome! Though I strongly encourage you to take the time to make your own lists, as it's helpful in assessing how you're feeling about your current intimate connections and how you'd like future ones to develop.

I use these criteria as my guiding principles when it comes to all bonds in my life, not just those with sexual or romantic intimacy. Should I have a relationship in my life that doesn't feel good in these ways, that's usually cause to pause. It's a sign that I need to check in with myself. Do I feel safe? Do I feel respected? Am I feeling sexy and desired? Am I being touched, talked to or engaged with in ways that make me feel good about myself? Do I feel like I can communicate my needs? The answers to these questions are pretty damn important and will either lead to happy affirmations about my connections or to important decisions for my mental health, wellness and safety. I hope that considering your own definitions and questions can help you figure these things out when it comes to the connections in your life—the ones you already have and any new ones you may develop over time. It's also normal for these criteria to change over time, so consider revisiting your thoughts on this topic regularly.

HOW TO CHECK IF YOUR RELATIONSHIP IS TRANS QUEER AFFIRMING

Just a friendly reminder that if your relationship feels invalidating to your identity, or if your partner is not fully supportive of who you are, or doesn't seem interested in making necessary changes to help you feel comfortable, or isn't respecting your pronouns or using the name and terms that you've asked them to use—chances are that your relationship is not trans queer affirming. Sadly, this situation can happen with trans queer folks just as it can with cisgender partners.

I once dated a girl who claimed to be supportive of trans and gender-nonconforming folks, but who constantly referred to me as "assigned male" (because I had a penis, you see), gave me compliments typically used for men, refused to touch or interact with my butt at all yet expected me to touch hers, and often got grumpy and annoyed with me whenever I was super cuddly and affectionate because that was "her job." Another time, I was hooking up with a gay guy who insisted that even after being with me, a nonbinary queer, he was a **gold star gay** who'd only ever had sex with men. He also wouldn't top or fuck me (because he was the bottom and needed an assertive man), and he never used singular they pronouns for me. Looking back, I don't believe he saw me as trans or nonbinary at all.

These were not trans queer–affirming relationships. They did not uplift, consider or respect who I was, and I chose to ignore many red flags because I didn't realize that things could be different.

Since these connections, I've learned a lot about what to look out for. I have even discovered a few green flags worth mentioning, like your partner making a concerted effort to use the language about you and your body that makes you feel happy, or changing the language they use to describe your relationship, or even themself, to reflect the fact that they hold your shared connection in high regard. For example, being gay is valid, but if a guy stops calling himself a "gold star gay" because he acknowledges that he has a nonbinary partner and experiences attraction to trans people who aren't strictly "men," that's some top-notch trans queer–affirming relationshipping in my book!

Here are some helpful questions you might want to ask yourself to judge whether your current connections are trans queer affirming:

1. Do you feel free to authentically be yourself without guilt, shame, arguments or like you're constantly being challenged?
2. Do you feel that your partner explicitly supports and respects your identity?
3. Does your partner use your correct pronouns?
4. Does your partner use language for and about you that is respectful and considerate of how you identify?
5. Do you feel good about the sex that you're having?
6. Is your partner genuinely interested and invested in ensuring your comfort within the relationship?
7. When your partner introduces you or talks about your relationship, do they do so in a way that makes you feel seen and celebrated, or do they seem hesitant and embarrassed?

Writing down your answers and working through them in a journal is one great way of processing what they may mean to you. Should you find yourself coming to a lot of negative conclusions, which reveal that some of your relationships may not be as safe, uplifting and supportive as you'd hoped they would be, you may want to consider reaching out to a trustworthy friend or talking to a mental health professional for guidance. If you feel comfortable talking to your partner or lover about how you are feeling, you may want to write down your thoughts and emotions ahead of time so you have them on hand before starting that conversation.

Sometimes in reflecting on our relationships in these ways, we come to difficult realizations about just how bad things have become. In the event that you find yourself feeling trapped or fearful for your mental health or physical safety, or unable to speak to your intimate partner without worrying about violence or other repercussions, I highly recommend that you attempt to reach a professional or confide in a safe friend or family member, and start considering what steps you need to take to leave that situation.

ALL THE WAYS THAT SEX AND PLEASURE CAN WORK

I think one of the problems we all face when it comes to these sorts of discussions, and to assessing our needs and wants around sexual intimacy, is that in our society, sex is widely presented as penetrative by nature. It's either cocks going into pussies, or dicks into buttholes, or fingers or toys into all sorts of orifices. But while penetrative sex can be pleasurable, there is such a diverse variety of ways to experience pleasure outside of penetration.

Sometimes pleasure doesn't even require anyone to get naked! Take dry humping, for example. Whether you're dressed in a full outfit or just your underwear, everything about the act of grinding yourself against somebody else while cuddling and making out can be supremely hot. Honestly, some of the best orgasms I've ever had occurred from firmly and passionately rubbing my erection against my partner's ass through our underwear early in the morning.

You can also rub your genitals directly against somebody else's. Whether you're stroking two dicks pressed together (often known as "**frotting**"), or grinding your clit against another clit, or sliding your cock up and down and around a **t-dick**, every possible combination of genitals can experience pleasure through this kind of stimulation. Using lube can also increase pleasure, decrease potential discomfort and help prevent even minor friction-related injuries.

If you're not interested in genital-to-genital contact, **mutual masturbation** is an often-overlooked option. While it's frequently treated as foreplay, it can be a satisfying and fulfilling form of sex in and of itself. Mutual masturbation can mean either masturbating each other or masturbating in front of one another. I'm a big fan of using the show-and-tell version of mutual masturbation as a means of showing your partner how you get off, while watching how they stimulate themself. Many of my partners and I have used mutual masturbation to express our needs and wants to one another, using the visual aid to demonstrate exactly what it is that brings us the most pleasure. It's a pretty empowering sexual communication tool, on top of just being really sexy!

To masturbate yourself or someone else, you can use your hands or any number of sex toys. For people with a penis, you can use masturbation sleeves, strokers or even a vibrating wand to stimulate the frenulum (the soft tissue along the underside of the penis, right below the head) and the rest of the shaft. Given that the prostate is a great source of sexual pleasure, you may also want to consider using a dildo or vibrator, or inserting an anal plug or prostate stimulator. For safety reasons, I highly recommend that you only explore anal play using toys with a wide, firm, flared base to minimize the risk of something getting caught up inside of you by accident. And I speak from experience: it happened to me several years ago while I was wearing a plug and running some errands. Let's just say I needed to make a very stressful stop in a public bathroom and I still feel extremely lucky that I was able to get it out myself. You don't want to experience that anxiety, trust me.

For people with a vulva and vagina, you can choose from tons of dildos, vibrators, rabbits, wands, massagers and clit stimulators. Exploring and experimenting with the size and shape of penetrating toys also allows you to figure out what gives you the most pleasure and hits all the right spots for you. And don't forget that you too have a butthole that, should you enjoy it, can also be a supreme source of sexual pleasure. If you're a furry or into pet play, you can also explore the wonder of tail plugs. And again, you can also just use your fingers for vaginal or anal penetration!

Sensation play and sensual touch are also great options to consider in place of penetrative sex. Maybe it's giving or receiving a deep and intimate full-body massage with (or without) sexual stimulation, or being blindfolded and having fingernails or other objects traced over your skin, or doing temperature play by slowly applying ice cubes to a person's erogenous zones or dripping hot wax over their stomach and chest. I'm a big fan of giving my husband a bath. Every so often, I'll run the water for him, put in some bubble bath, dim the lights, maybe play some sexy music, and overall make it nice and calming. Then I'll soap him up and wash him from head to toe! Oftentimes, that's where it stops, and it feels like a thoroughly fulfilling intimate experience for us both, but sometimes I might also masturbate him while he's in the tub, or we take it to the bedroom for more play, though that's never an expectation.

You can also do much of this masturbation and sensation play alone. Anybody can use toys on themselves, or carefully enjoy solo kink. You can experiment with pain, pleasure and sensation play all on your own. There's nothing weird about spanking yourself with a paddle, be it on your ass or thighs, and it's totally normal to wear a collar or leather cuffs while masturbating or teasing yourself with various items and fabrics. Hell, go ahead and blindfold or gag yourself if you'd like! Just be sure to do so safely by using a breathable silicone ball gag, and avoid using any items or fabrics that may obstruct your airway or lead to a dangerous choking hazard. The great thing about taking the time to bring yourself pleasure is that you can touch and interact with yourself in any way you want to, which makes you the most trans queer–affirming partner you could ever possibly have.

Selphie Labrys and Aviva Romelli star in
Crash Pad Series **"Episode 216."**

KINK AND BDSM DYNAMICS

BDSM, kinks and power dynamics present a whole world to explore. While often quite sexual and sensual, these often-complex forms of intimacy can also be entirely emotional and physical without a heavy focus on sex. Many folks who are **aroace**—meaning somebody who is both asexual and aromantic—find a lot of enjoyment in BDSM because it allows them to develop deeply intimate bonds and experience a wide range of pleasure without the pressure or expectations of being sexual in traditional ways.

If pain is your thing, you could find yourself somebody to Dom or top you for a session of impact play (spanking, caning, slapping, hitting, whipping and so on) with various instruments such as canes, floggers, whips, paddles or other body-safe implements. These sessions can be one-off experiences, or done with a Master or owner as part of an established relationship. Or maybe you want to be the one doling out the pain!

Role-play—in addition to pain play, or on its own—can include fantasy situations such as medical play, submission and service connections, or even hardcore but consensual non-consent scenarios.

Bondage often goes hand in hand with many of the above scenarios. You can buy yourself some handcuffs and rope for this practice, or use implements you may already have in your home, which can be as simple as a necktie, scarves, stockings, shirts, long socks, or even torn strips of towels or blankets. Just be sure to think about safety at all times. Never tie somebody up and leave them unattended for long, or tie them too tightly, which can cut off circulation and cause injury. And never attempt any form of hanging bondage, or breath play, without thoroughly educating yourself on the risks and best practices.

Personally, I'm an enormous fan of pet play. Here's a bit about how this looks in my life. I have collared my husband Fenric as my pup, and I've named him Howl. As his owner, I look after him in as many ways as I can. I love giving him baths, head scritches and body massages; hand-feeding him; taking him for walkies on his leash; giving him cuddles and affirmations; and breeding him nice and deep whenever I want. It's all about creating a safe space where I can worship and treat him like the good pup he is, so that he desires his Master's cum and cock. As my pup, he gives me free use of himself for my sexual and emotional pleasure as much as is reasonable, and I never take that for granted.

For others, pet play might also include an owner having their pet stay in a dog kennel, sleep in a pet bed, or even eat out of bowls on the floor. Some dynamics could even involve more primal aspects, such as predator/prey relationships with sexual sessions involving the submissive being hunted by the Dominant, whether around the house or outside.

Shibari, a type of rope bondage also known as kinbaku, is another kink I often see trans queer folks engage in. Based on Japanese rope-tying practices, shibari can be kinky, artistic or even meditative in its execution. Literally translating as "to tie/bind," it's a collaborative experience between a rigger (the person doing the tying up) and a rope bunny (the person being tied up). Shibari may involve a degree of BDSM dynamics, but it can also simply be a vulnerable exploration of the body. Many people enjoy it sexually, including as foreplay or in explicitly sexual play scenes, but I've also seen countless individuals engage in the act for the sensations, relaxation and connection it also provides. You can even keep most of your clothes on, and ask that your genitals, breasts or other erogenous zones be avoided entirely while focusing instead on your arms, legs, hips, waist or other areas. Perhaps shibari could even become a part of your sexy look, as you have rope harnesses applied to your chest or entire torso and genitals. Or maybe it's more of a thing you lay back and enjoy, closing your eyes as your partner experiments with different types of ties that result in a wide range of constriction sensations.

Depending on your desires, you can develop all sorts of kinky bonds as you explore these dynamics. It just takes some creativity, strong boundaries and clear communication!

Puck Goodfellow and Ari Koyote star in
Crash Pad Series **"Episode 354."**

THINKING OUTSIDE OF THE BOX

Sex can also work very differently from the cishet template in lots of other ways. For example, there's a big misconception that one must be partially or entirely naked to have sex, and that those involved need to physically interact with one another. But that's just wrong. You don't even need to be in the same damn room as the other person for you to be having sex together.

Sexting, for example, allows you to explore a wide range of eroticism, fantasy and pleasuré through your phone or laptop from the privacy of your bedroom. Sexting can range from sending somebody long, detailed horny messages that essentially read as short-form erotica, to describing all of the incredibly filthy things you would be doing with them if they were there with you, or even to taking a bunch of lewds and nudes, maybe a few short sexy video clips, and sending them back and forth while you compliment and dirty talk with one another. This act can lead to you masturbating over video together, or on a voice call, or on your own between intermittent texting. It can also lead to no masturbation at all, instead just serving as something exciting and playful that doesn't need to end in an orgasm in order to be enjoyable.

Sex in person also doesn't have to follow a typical playbook. You can remain fully clothed, and you don't need to touch the other person while you're in the same physical space. I know lots of folks who enjoy watching others have sex in person while they masturbate on their own in the same room, or even wait until it's done and masturbate in private. As I mentioned in the last section, mutual masturbation also allows several folks in the same room to stimulate themselves with their hands, or all manner of sex toys, without engaging with one another at all if they don't want to.

Lots of individuals also love giving sexual pleasure, but not necessarily receiving it themselves, and that's valid too! I was once with somebody who loved to give me oral sex, jerk me off while fingering my butt, use sex toys on me, or just watch me masturbate while I leaned against them or laid beside them. They enjoyed it when I humped their leg or their butt through leggings or panties, and I remember how their face would light up when I orgasmed and ejaculated. They'd smile, ask if they did good, and then giggle and do this little wiggle to express their pride in their sexy skills when I told them how good and sexy they made me feel. Yet they never wanted me to give them oral or aid them in achieving an orgasm in return. What they needed instead was to cuddle, get head pats and gently make out after they got me off, and then they went home.

So if you're having trouble figuring out what feels good and right for you, just know that you don't have to have sex or be sexually active in any of the ways you have before, or any of the ways you think you should. Sex in media, and especially in porn—even the trans queer stuff—has a tendency to rely heavily on intercourse and mostly depicts very standard, traditional forms of play. You don't have to do any of that if you don't enjoy it, and there are countless other ways for you to creatively explore and share in pleasure with others.

Chocolate Chip and Eros LaFemme star in *Crash Pad Series* "Episode 219."

INTIMACY AND PLEASURE WITHOUT PRESSURE FOR SEX

Not wanting or desiring sex or sexual activity is also valid! You can experience physical intimacy in a ton of different ways that don't involve intercourse of any kind. Making out, kissing and licking, hugging, cuddling, spanking, groping, and even some more controlled dry humping and grinding can all provide pleasurable sensations. You're absolutely within your right to engage in the activities that feel good and comfortable to you, without having to do anything else. Ultimately, you can define for yourself what sex is, and what it isn't.

You aren't alone if you don't want sex. A great deal of people don't! Perhaps they are asexual, aromantic, both or neither. They may have some sexual trauma and anxieties and prefer not to be sexually active. Or maybe it's just something they don't want right now, but might again someday. The point is that if you wish to find others who crave physical intimacy without it leading to more, they are out there and you can find them. Just remember to clearly communicate your needs, wants, boundaries and expectations.

Should you find yourself with somebody who seems to be having a lot of difficulty respecting your limits—perhaps they have begun to push you, try to guilt or shame you, become physically aggressive, or ignore your stated boundaries—I implore you to look out for yourself and take the steps you need to keep safe. Even if that means ending that connection. You deserve to have your consent and body respected under all circumstances, and sharing physical intimacy with somebody in no way entitles them to have sex with you.

Devon Wipp and Milo Elizabeth star in
Crash Pad Series **"Episode 201."**

QUEERING YOUR VOCABULARY: INCLUSIVE WORDS FOR YOUR GENITALS AND OTHER BODY PARTS

One of the most essential ways of reclaiming autonomy over myself as a trans queer was redefining the language I use to describe my body. Some of the ways that I had referred to my genitals and other physical parts of myself just didn't feel right anymore, and since I wasn't transitioning from one binary gender to another, just switching from male descriptors to female ones wouldn't work either. As a lewd, rude, gender-fucking queer with a penis, I needed words that were appropriately empowering, gay as fuck and subversive as hell to refer to my body.

For a solid several years, I referred to my penis as my girl cock. It felt affirming for a time, and I enjoyed the looks of excitement on the faces of my partners and lovers as they said it. It also made cishets angry, as many saw fit to come to my blog and leave frustrated comments about how I "can't do that" and am "just making words up," which was delightful to me, if I'm being honest. Nowadays I just use the word "cock," which feels good for me in my more recent understanding of my identity as genderfaun, with my sense of self existing fluidly between nonbinary and some form of queer masculinity, rather than anything overtly feminine. But queering your language is still a blast!

You may already have heard some standard trans queer—specific descriptors, and I've used some of them earlier in this book. For trans men and trans masc folks, you tend to hear some combination of dick, cock, t-dick, clit dick or click, dicklet, bonus hole, front hole, boy pussy/

cunt or bussy (which is also sometimes used by queer men for their butthole). For trans girls, the most common terms are clit, girl dick, clit dick, femme/fem cock and my personal favourite, hen, the opposite of a cock. Adorable, right? Various portmanteaus exist as well, though some are considered slightly more controversial as they have also been used in a more derogatory manner. These include terms such as mangina, pengina, venis and shenis, each of which has been reclaimed and proudly used by many trans queers.

Pet names are also a lot of fun, and many of them can easily be used as gender-neutral descriptors. These can include bedfellow, nethers, tenders, precious, muff, puppet, minion, turtle, toy, fellow traveller, consort, instigator, inciter, beast, monster, fuck or sex. Try them out with your partner while dirty talking to see if any feel good to you! For example, while having oral performed on you, tell them to "suck my fuck" or "take my beast." Maybe one of these words clicks, maybe not, but it can be fun exploring them!

Or just keep to the basics! Apart from the classic dick, cock, pussy, cunt, penis and vagina, you have a range of simple options. Consider crotch, member, parts, bits, junk, privates, goods, stuff, unit, equipment, area, below, down-stairs, undercarriage or just your business. Throw in an adjective too, if you want to get creative with it—try dirty goods, pleasure parts, fun button or sexy funtime zone. Whatever works best for you!

You can also use honorifics, either for yourself or partners, such as in a kink or intimate dynamic, or for your genitals. I've heard a wide range of titles applied in both contexts, such as captain, boss, Master, chancellor or emissary. For some extra subversiveness, try highness, excellency, esquire or even holiness. Or get creative and hop on that online gaming name generator you love to get ideas for your "fearless hero," "guardian of my pants" or "herald of orgasms"!

There are no rules. Have fun with the process and use whatever words you want.

The key is that you get to do so for yourself. As wonderful as it is to develop your own language for yourself and your body, deciding for others or forcing words onto them isn't OK. One of the worst intimate experiences I ever had early in my coming out was, unfortunately, with a trans woman who insisted that I was, in fact, also a woman, despite me not identifying as such. Throughout our second, and last, play session together, she called me a sissy, told me I could be a "good girl" for her, used several feminine terms to refer to my body and told me how pretty I'd be once I "started on HRT," all while knowing that I was actually nonbinary and had made no such transition decisions for myself, as I wasn't yet sure what I actually wanted. The whole experience left a bad taste in my mouth, and I did not invite her over again.

Sadly, at that time, my communication skills weren't as strong as they are now and I did not speak up for myself, instead opting to let our time together fizzle out and to then simply keep my distance. But should you find yourself in a similar situation and want to keep that connection, you are well within your rights to correct the terminology your partner or lover is using for you, even if they too are trans queer. Nobody gets to decide for you how to refer to your body.

Be it in person, or over text or other messages, it's always best to start the conversation as directly as possible. Send something along the lines of "I really enjoy playing together, however, I've been feeling uncomfortable about some of the words used for my body and would like to talk about it when you have the time." If they don't respond well to that comment, or if they become defensive or ignore it, you can decide for yourself if you want to keep pursuing that connection.

Remember, you don't have to have a full conversation with anyone who has made you feel uncomfortable! It's also OK to simply end a connection that you disliked. You don't owe anyone a second chance, an explanation or any particular form of communication. Contrary to the popular notion that you have to speak to somebody in person or over the phone to end a relationship of any kind, I strongly feel that if it's best for your safety and mental health to send a text, then you go right ahead and text it.

WHERE TO FIND TRANS QUEER-AFFIRMING PORN

We touched on it a little in chapter 1, but just to reiterate: porn has a long history of being quite toxic in its approach. It tends to focus on the cis male gaze, with content revolving around the pleasure of cishet men while cishet women, and even cis queer men, exist only to serve as glorified sex toys. When trans people are present, they are often referred to with derogatory slurs and treated as fun, unique, experiments for the star of a scene to dominate, or be dominated by, after which the star quickly moves on. Overall, the porn industry is rife with sexism, racism, queerphobia, transphobia and ableism, as well as toxic body standards, depictions of unsafe sex practices and the fetishization of nonconsensual sex. Many of us who discovered porn at a young age probably didn't pick up much positivity from it; at best, it may have encouraged us to hold ourselves to unrealistic sexual ideals, and at worst, it may have taught us some really bad behaviours.

So, why bother watching porn at all?

Well, it turns out that tons of trans queer–affirming adult content is now available. It's made by, and for, trans queer people, and the spirit of diversity, inclusion and radical acceptance permeates it all! Trans queer porn is filmed, edited and sold by trans queer performers, and it shows them exploring their pleasure and sexuality in safe, affirming ways. It shows diverse body types, doesn't use dehumanizing terms or slurs, and contains no weirdly cisnormative or heteronormative objectification. It's just radical self-love and radical trans queer pleasure and joy. Do recommend!

Of course, if porn makes you uncomfortable, and you don't enjoy any of it—even amateur content created consensually by trans queer performers—that's OK. However, if you're open to checking out more inclusive, sex- and body-positive content, you may actually learn a lot about yourself! One of the best things about trans queer–created adult content is that it includes far more creative and unique explorations of sex, sexuality and sexual pleasure. By watching trans queer amateur porn, I learned how to suck t-dick better and discovered more ways to touch and pleasure trans women. I also discovered cool ways of making myself ejaculate, such as from hands-free prostate orgasms and using vibrators to stimulate my frenulum. I never would have known about these skills and options otherwise.

Amateur trans queer erotic content also helped me unpack a lot of shame I had internalized about being fat, queer and aging. It even went a long way toward destigmatizing some of my less common kinks, which is great because opening up to my partners about them has allowed me to experience a far more fulfilling sex life.

Finding this kind of porn can be a little overwhelming at first, but two pretty reliable sources can help you seek out this content. First, a number of revolutionary queer porn studios and streaming services have been making outstanding content since the early 2010s. These studios and sites were founded and are run by trans queer performers and sex work activists such as Jiz Lee, Shine Louise Houston, Courtney Trouble, Chelsea Poe and Vanniall, to name just a few. The best part is that the sites all tend to work together, linking to and promoting each other's content. As such, you can quickly discover whole networks of fairly priced sites where you can purchase individual films and scenes from a diverse list of performers, or pay an ongoing subscription fee for access. Many of these sites feature not only trans queers, but also fat, disabled and BIPOC performers.

The second major source of outstanding trans queer erotic content is social media. Many performers run their own user accounts where they post short video clips, photos and links to sites where you can purchase more of their content. The trick is in knowing what terms and tags to search. Frustratingly, they tend to change and evolve over time, but you're likely to find success by searching for the more standard stuff such as #transporn, #transnsfw,

#ftmnsfw, #mtfnsfw, #tdick, #boypussy and similar trans queer terminology. Heads up that you are also likely to find some folks using potentially triggering terms and reclaimed slurs here.

Using those same search terms on various porn tube sites will also bring you to trans queer content creators making awesome work. Sadly, a lot of these mainstream sites continue to use transphobic slurs as category titles, and several trans porn studios rely on queerphobic framing niches to market predominantly to cishet men, rather than trans queer viewers. While the porn industry has made many strides over the years, the industry as a whole—including practically all of the bigger free tube sites such as Pornhub, XVideos and xHamster—hasn't done much to make pornography accessible to marginalized users or done anything to change harmful tropes about trans queers. Be aware that while searching for trans and nonbinary queer porn can help you find cool creators, using these search terms on mainstream tube sites is also likely to expose you to the use of degrading slurs and transphobic tropes.

If you'd like some direct links to sites and creators I recommend, be sure to check the resources section at the back of this book.

MAKING THE CONTENT YOU WANT TO SEE

Depending on your comfort level, I also recommend you consider creating your own sexual spaces for your interested partners, friends and community peers. When I started blogging at mxnillin.com over a decade ago, I was genuinely surprised to discover how many people I knew who, like me, felt extremely sexually repressed in their lives as trans queers and who desired the opportunity and safe space to share their own nudes and see nudes from other trans queer people. Over the years, I've created and moderated Discord servers, Facebook Messenger groups, Telegram channels and other group chats of various sizes—from just a handful of folks to hundreds of members.

Nowadays I mostly post to my site, or to my very NSFW social media, but I have also maintained a handful of connections online with friends with whom I'll trade nudes and provide affirmations and hype about how hot and amazing they look in their **thirst pics**. This level of ethical exhibitionism and voyeurism with people I trust, who will use my pronouns and the language that's most comfortable for me while complimenting my body, goes a long way in helping me feel seen as attractive in truly affirming and empowering ways.

You can do the same by cultivating connections with like-minded people you already know, and even with those you've yet to meet online or in your local community. Some good first steps are to create NSFW accounts for yourself on social media platforms that allow them, or reach out to your closer friends who you think might be more open-minded about nude trading. Posting on some of the trans queer–friendly Reddit forums is a great way to start putting yourself out there to connect more intimately online with others! Be mindful, though, that not all of those forums are moderated in harm-reducing ways, and some users may share potentially hurtful ideals such as transmedicalism and "real trans" rhetoric. If it's not feeling affirming or safe, listen to your gut and disengage!

If you're seriously considering posting or sharing nudes, be sure that you don't take that decision lightly. Once they're out there, nudes are nearly impossible to take back, even when you share them with partners or friends. While it's obviously abhorrent behaviour, it's not uncommon for bitter exes and angry former friends to repost or share intimate photos they received in the past. Sharing somebody's nudes without permission is inexcusable and if someone does this to you, it would not be your fault, of course. But it can, and does, happen.

If you want to be more public about posting nudes while also protecting your identity, you can take a few precautions. Don't include your face, don't take explicit photos in a space that's easily recognizable as your own (watch for photos or art in the background), and do your best to obscure or avoid any identifiable tattoos, scars, birthmarks, moles and so on.

If, much like me, you aren't concerned about protecting your identity, it's also valid to just put yourself out there uncensored! Let your sex- and body-positive flag fly however it feels best to you! Just understand that you need to be comfortable with the fact that anyone you know, and I mean absolutely anyone—including your parents, other family members and colleagues—could potentially come across those images someday.

CONCLUSION
EIGHT IMPORTANT TAKEAWAYS

I've said a lot about a wide range of topics over the last several chapters, but if I were to narrow down what I hope you take away from reading this book, it's these eight key points:

1. It's incredibly hard to feel sexy, or even to understand how you may be perceived as sexy by others, in a world that almost always centres thin, white, cisgender and heterosexual individuals as the standard for "hotness." While you have no control over societal standards, try your best to not let them rule you. It's not your fault that you've been struggling to feel desirable amid the pressures and expectations for love and acceptance as dictated by cishet society. You're doing your best, and you'll find what you're looking for in time.

2. Unlearning traditional gender roles and expectations, challenging toxic monogamy culture and unpacking your own queerphobic and transphobic baggage from your upbringing is all part of the process for finding your sexy. While it's not easy to acknowledge, the fact is that we've all been conditioned throughout our lives to see trans queer identities and bodies as strange and undesirable. It's important to focus our efforts

on challenging this perception so that we don't cause unintentional harm, either to ourselves or others.

3. "Sexy" is hard to define because what each individual finds attractive is subjective and unique. In addition, we can experience attraction in myriad ways, including sexual, romantic, aesthetic and physical, sometimes all at once and other times independently.

4. Showing yourself patience and empathy goes a long way in helping you create a safe, affirming, encouraging and uplifting environment and state of mind for finding your sexy. You are allowed to take as much time as you need with this process, and it's OK to make mistakes along the way.

5. Wanting to feel sexy does not necessarily have to be tied to any need for sexual activity, or any form of relationship with others. It can be as much about building up your own self-worth, redefining or exploring who you are on intimate emotional and physical levels, and feeling affirmed within yourself.

6. There is no right or wrong way to "be" sexy, just as there is no right or wrong way to be trans queer. You're allowed to change your mind about things. You're allowed to experiment, explore and switch things up as much or as little as you want to. You're allowed to change the language you use to describe yourself, your experiences and your body, as much as you need to. You're allowed to say no. You're allowed to say yes. Only you have any say in how this journey is going to go for you.

7. Before you start exploring more intimate connections with others, take the time to understand your own

personal needs, wants, boundaries and nonnegotiables as best you can. Identifying what's important to you helps a great deal in avoiding boundary violations, conflict, disappointment and other miscommunication issues.

8. Sometimes, discovering the connections and community you desire involves building spaces and opportunities for that discovery to occur in the ways you need it to. If the available options don't feel right for you, don't hesitate to forge new paths. You'd be surprised at how many others might feel similarly and would join you in those efforts.

Overall, I hope you know how valid and important your happiness, pleasure, safety and fulfillment are. It isn't selfish to prioritize and celebrate yourself. In fact, I believe it is imperative! By taking the time to find your sexy, to understand your needs, to communicate better with yourself and others, and to foster empowering connections, you're living the life that countless other trans queers have fought so hard for us all to have. This is what it's all about, folks. Valuing yourself, living authentically and empowering those around you, all while getting and giving the most you can with what little time we have here.

You've got this. You're worth the work and effort.

GLOSSARY

ableism. Discrimination toward people with disabilities (physical, psychological, intellectual, developmental or learning-related). Ableism stems from the assumption that disabled people are somehow broken, weak, incapable or otherwise inferior, and in need of somehow being fixed.

ACAB. An abbreviation for all cops are bastards. Because they are.

ADHD. An abbreviation for attention deficit hyperactivity disorder. A neurological condition in which an individual experiences a range of struggles with memory, focus, impulsivity, time management, hyperactivity, emotional regulation and more.

AFAB. An abbreviation for assigned female at birth. Describes when a baby is born and a doctor looks at its genitals and goes "ah, a vagina," and then writes "female" on the baby's birth certificate. This assignment then informs how that child is raised and socialized.

agender. A gender identity or, alternatively, a statement to express a person's lack of any gender at all.

alt-right. A white nationalist, anti-LGBTQ+, far-right ideological movement that's mostly based online. Since the early 2000s, alt-righters have worked hard to disseminate bigoted misinformation of many kinds, promote anti-Semitic conspiracy theories, denounce all forms of mainstream media, and stoke fear and hatred of newcomers and trans queer people.

amatonormativity. The cultural assumption that all human beings want to pursue romantic bonds, find a single romantic partner and enter into a long-term monogamous relationship with that person.

ambigender. A gender identity in which the individual experiences two genders simultaneously, with no fluidity or shifting between them. Can fall under the bigender or multigender umbrella.

androgynous. A form of gender expression in which somebody's behaviours and presentation incorporate a mix of masculinity and femininity, or an absence of either.

aroace. Combining the short forms for the identities *aromantic* and *asexual*, this term describes a person who is both.

aromantic. An identity for somebody who experiences little or no romantic desire or attraction. Aromantic people still enjoy deeply fulfilling relationships that may also include affection, sensuality or sex, but don't feel the need to partake in romantic activities.

asexual. An identity for somebody who does not experience sexual attraction to others or desire for sexual experiences. Asexuality does not necessarily mean that someone doesn't enjoy sexual pleasure at all. Some asexual people can be sex-repulsed, wanting nothing to do with sex whatsoever; others may be indifferent to sex, feeling neither repulsed by or positive about sex, or even sex-favourable, meaning that while they may not experience sexual attraction, they still enjoy having sex.

BDSM. A catch-all phrase that describes the activities, interpersonal relationships and power dynamics of people involved in a wide variety of kinky erotic practices. The acronym specifically refers to the practices of bondage and discipline (B/D), Dominance and submission (D/s), and sadism and masochism (S/M).

BIPOC. An abbreviation for Black, Indigenous and people of colour.

butch. An identity that emerged from within lesbian and bisexual culture and was used to describe a woman with a more masculine identity or gender presentation. Butch has since evolved as a label and is used by some *nonbinary* people, as well as *queer* individuals of various sexual orientations.

cam site. A website where sex workers, adult performers and/or models are able to live stream themselves and earn tips from viewers. These sites are often publicly viewable, but after receiving a set amount of tips, performers may change their settings to private to put on an intimate, often sexually explicit show for those who paid.

campy. An adjective describing queer self-expressions that are particularly exaggerated, outspoken, loud and otherwise considered "over the top" and "out there." Camp has a long history and a range of meanings that no short definition can hope to encapsulate—it's a wonderful rabbit hole to go down if you want to learn more!

cis. The short form of the word *cisgender*.

cisgender. An identity for somebody who isn't *trans* or *nonbinary*. They were assigned a gender at birth based on their perceived sex, were then socialized as such, and have continued to identify with that gender.

cishet. The shorthand way of referring to somebody who is both *cisgender* and heterosexual.

cisnormative/cisnormativity. The widespread assumption that everyone identifies as the gender they were assigned at birth. Acts as a structural barrier for *trans* and *gender-diverse* people in all areas of their life, as society functions without consideration for them. Cisnormativity is often one issue at the core of *transphobia* and *queerphobia*.

C-PTSD. An abbreviation for complex post-traumatic stress disorder. Describes a range of long-term symptoms such as panic attacks, anxiety, severe depression, re-experiencing traumatic memories (emotional flashbacks), repeated stress nightmares and being easily startled; feeling tense and on edge, angry, afraid, guilty, ashamed and dissociated; and having difficulty sleeping or staying awake, focusing and controlling emotions. PTSD is complex when the cause of these symptoms is deeply rooted in sustained trauma such as childhood abuse, ongoing domestic violence, or repeatedly witnessing violence or abuse, among other experiences.

crossdresser. An individual who wears clothing associated with gender identities and expressions that are not typical of their assigned sex. While crossdressing has historically been understood in the context of *cisgender* men wearing feminine clothing, it can encompass a much broader range of expression; for example, it can apply to *nonbinary* individuals dressing in binary or other *gender-nonconforming* ways.

Daddy. A kink honorific used by some *submissives* for their *Dominant*, who role-plays as a paternalistic authority figure.

date friend. A friend who you sometimes go out on dates with. These dates are mostly platonic in nature, and work to further nurture your friendship, but they can also include romance and/or sex, as well as other forms of physical and emotional intimacy that may not be easily categorized as things that "just friends" do.

deadnaming. The act of calling a *trans* person by the name they were given at birth, which they no longer use as it causes them pain and discomfort, rather than calling them by their chosen name. Regardless of intent, it is transphobic to deadname a trans person.

demigender. A gender identity describing an individual who identifies partially, but not wholly, with a specific gender identity, or gender in general. Can also serve as an umbrella term for such individuals.

Dominant/Dom/Domme. The individual in control of a *BDSM* dynamic or scene. Dominants take charge and top their *submissive* in a consensual power exchange. A good, safe Dominant listens to their submissive, considers their safety, communicates with them and actively checks in with them during play. When written, the first letter of each of these words is usually capitalized to denote the person's authority role in a dynamic.

dyke. Originally a homophobic slur used to harm lesbian women, the term has been reclaimed by many lesbians in a positive way to celebrate their identity.

dysphoria. The experience of discomfort, dread or unhappiness with one's assigned gender. Many, but not all, *trans* folks experience a deep disconnect between their physical and psychological selves, which causes severe distress. To align themselves physically with how they perceive themselves internally, trans people often desire to transition socially and sometimes medically or surgically as well.

Eagle. Many gay bars worldwide, especially leather-, kink- and *BDSM*-focused ones, have been called "The Eagle" or have used "Eagle" in their names. It is commonly seen in *queer* communities as signaling that an establishment is safe and welcoming of kinksters.

enby. The phonetic pronunciation of "NB," the short form of *nonbinary*. Can be used as a term of endearment or a relational title in place of more binary words such as aunt or uncle, mom or dad, brother or sister.

enboy. The combination of the words *enby* and boy. Can refer to somebody who identifies as a *nonbinary* man, or as both male and nonbinary, or somebody whose identity is some degree of nonbinary and some degree of boy.

ey/em/emself. Pronouns used by some *trans* individuals. Derived from they/them/themself, but dropping the "th."

femboy. Somebody who identifies as a boy but presents himself very femininely through clothing, hair, makeup and mannerisms.

feminization. In the context of this book, feminization refers to the practice of dressing femininely and presenting as more feminine in an intimate context. Frequently a form of *BDSM* play, with a *Dom* applying makeup to their *submissive* and dressing them in lingerie or other feminine attire. For some, it is part of a consensual "forced" role-play. Feminization may also be referred to as "*sissification.*"

femme. A gender identity and a term used to more broadly describe a range of feminine and feminine-adjacent gender expressions.

fetish. An object, activity or body part that an individual experiences an extreme degree of sexual desire for and sexual gratification from.

folx. A term often used in place of "folks" to be explicitly inclusive of marginalized groups and individuals. It was popular for a time within *queer* spaces and writing, though its usage can be controversial as some people consider it to be performative virtue signalling without doing any work to actually be inclusive.

frotting. The sexual act of rubbing, holding, masturbating or otherwise sexually stimulating two or more penises together.

FTM. An abbreviation for female to male.

furries. People who are interested in anthropomorphic animal characters. They may dress up as these characters in *fursuits* or commission art of the characters.

fursona. An anthropomorphic animal persona adopted by *furries*. A furry may have one or more fursonas.

fursuit. A custom-made animal costume, often designed to represent the wearer's *fursona*. These suits can be full, meaning they consist of a head, paws, bodysuit and feet, or partial, meaning they consist of a head with or without paws, a tail and feet. Many fursuits are made from a variety of fabrics such as fur, foam and fleece.

gender binary. In the context of this book, and most discussion of gender identity, the binary refers to the social notion that there exist only two genders, man and woman (or boy and girl); two forms of gender expression, masculine and feminine; and two sexes, male and female. This belief also states that each person embodies only one set, meaning a male person identifies as a man and is masculine, and a female person identifies as a woman and is feminine. Most of society operates under the gender binary and it is at the core of most transphobic beliefs.

gender critical. A buzzword frequently used by *TERFs* and other anti-trans individuals to minimize their transphobic rhetoric and create a fake sense of safety and ease in others. You will often hear anti-trans activists claim that they are not transphobic, they are just "gender critical." However, at their core, gender-critical activists are opposed to the rights, protections, inclusion and humanity of *trans* and *gender-diverse* people.

gender diverse. A term that describes people who are not *cisgender* and express their gender identity outside of the *gender binary*.

gender essentialism. The toxic and harmful belief that specific traits inherently and exclusively belong to either men or women. Includes a lot of sexist notions such as thinking that all men are physically stronger than all women, or that women are naturally just better parents than men.

gender-fucking. The act of radically subverting social roles and expectations around the *gender binary* by fucking around with your identity and expression.

genderfaun. A form of gender fluidity that does not encompass any woman-aligned or feminine identities—unless those feminine traits and experiences align with masculine identity. Genderfaun individuals may also sometimes experience being genderless and express this identity through androgyny or gender nonconformity.

genderfluid. A gender identity that varies or changes over time, which may be daily, weekly, monthly, or from moment to moment.

gender nonconforming. The act of not conforming to, and often actively subverting and challenging, gender roles and expectations.

genderqueer. A gender identity that centres the "queering" of gender expression and expectations in a transgressive way. Often also used as an umbrella term similar to *nonbinary*, to encompass identities outside of binary standards.

gold star gay/lesbian. A self-descriptive term typically used by *cis* gay and lesbian individuals to express that they have only ever been attracted to and intimate with people who are of the same sex as them. It is a problematic term in that it can be transphobic, as some consider the title "lost" if somebody has had sex with a *trans* or *nonbinary* person. Sometimes used to implicitly denigrate those whose sexuality is broader or who are exploring or questioning their sexuality.

heteronormative/heteronormativity. The worldview that presents heterosexuality as the "normal," preferred and default sexual orientation for everyone. Heteronormativity informs and impacts all aspects of our society, often leading to policies, laws and social practices that invalidate and exclude nonheterosexuals. Heteronormativity is a core element of *queerphobia*.

HRT. An abbreviation for "hormone replacement therapy." A form of medical transition in which an individual takes prescribed doses of either estrogen or testosterone to achieve changes in their body affected by hormone levels.

While many take HRT to relieve symptoms of *dysphoria*, one does not need to be dysphoric to start on HRT.

hysterectomy. The surgical removal of the uterus. People who have a hysterectomy are then unable to get pregnant and will no longer have periods.

incel. A short form of "involuntarily celibate," a term popularized by an online-based ideological movement of extremely resentful *cishet* men who blame women and society as a whole for their lack of romantic success. They hold deeply misogynistic opinions, and often see all women as evil, promiscuous and holding far more power than they should. They believe themselves to be victims of feminism who have had their lives ruined by the women who have rejected them. Several high-profile incels have perpetrated mass shootings and killings over the years.

kings. Artists who dress in masculine drag and perform hypermasculinity, primarily through costume, character, dance and lip-synching.

LGBTQ+. An abbreviation for lesbian, gay, bisexual, *transgender*, *queer* and other sexual and gender-diverse individuals. Also sometimes written as LGBTQIA+ to explicitly include intersex and *asexual* people.

mammoplasty. A surgical operation that changes the shape, size or position of one or both breasts.

mastectomy. The surgical removal of all breast tissue from the body. While typically done to prevent breast cancer, it is also a common gender-affirming procedure.

microaggressions. A wide range of subtle comments or actions that express prejudice toward people of a given demographic. These can be very direct, but are also commonly done quite unconsciously. Intentional or not, microaggressions are very harmful and pervasive throughout society.

misgendering. The act of referring to somebody's gender incorrectly, for instance by using the wrong pronouns. Misgendering can be done on purpose or unintentionally. Regardless, it causes harm and is well known to be a transphobic act.

MTF. An abbreviation for male to female.

mutual masturbation. A sexual activity in which two or more individuals masturbate in front of each other, or masturbate one another with their hands or sex toys.

neutrois. A term to describe folks who do not see themselves in relation to the *gender binary* and often feel that they do not even have a gender identity to express. Sometimes also referred to as being gender neutral or genderless.

nonbinary. A gender identity that does not fit the *gender binary* system. Individuals may use this term to indicate that they don't adhere or relate to the gender binary or any of the identities and expressions that it encompasses. Also used as an umbrella term.

nonmonogamous. Describes someone who is not monogamous. People who are nonmonogamous typically have, or are open to having, more than one romantic or sexual partner. They may also primarily be in one committed relationship that allows for sexual freedom in having occasional hookups with others, group sex or other sexual experiences outside of that bond. Not everyone who is nonmonogamous is *polyamorous*; people who are in committed monogamous relationships may sometimes explore nonmonogamy through occasional group sex or other sexual activities with others from outside their relationship, but it is not typically a consistent practice.

NSFW. An abbreviation for not safe for work. Typically used to indicate that a given piece of content (such as a message, photo, video or link) is sexually explicit and should not be viewed in a workplace setting or anywhere where others may be exposed to sensitive content.

olfactophilia. Sexual arousal from bodily smells, such as sweat or the scent of genitals.

orchiectomy. The surgical removal of the testes.

pet play. A form of sexual role-play, and frequently a dynamic exchange, in which a *Dominant* serves as the Master and/or owner of their pet, a *submissive*. These roles can be static, but some pet players may also enjoy switching back and forth. Play often includes the sub being trained, punished, and treated as a pup, kitten or other domesticated animal. Many pets are collared by their owners, and they may wear their collar at all times to signify their dynamic, or only during play. They are also usually given a unique pet name by their owner, or the pet and owner may choose a name together.

play friend. A friend who you play with sexually or in the context of kink (also known as a scene partner). Can denote a close friend with benefits or just a casual pal you get off with on occasion.

polyamory. The practice of having multiple consensual and informed romantic, sexual or intimate emotional relationships. Polyamory is ethical when everybody is aware of one another, *safer sex* practices are discussed and adhered to, and everyone's boundaries are considered and respected.

pre-op. An abbreviation that refers to a *trans*, *nonbinary* or *gender-nonconforming* person who has not yet undergone, but intends to have, gender-affirming surgery.

pup hood. A hood made of leather, neoprene or a combination and shaped to look like a dog's head that is worn as part of *pet play*.

QAnon. A far-right political movement (with no explicit organization) centred in baseless, outlandish and often deeply anti-Semitic and racist conspiracies.

QTPOC. An abbreviation for queer and trans people of colour.

queens. Artists who dress in feminine drag and perform hyperfemininity, primarily through costume, character, dance and lip-synching.

queer. A reclaimed slur now most commonly used as an umbrella term. Queer, for those who choose to use it, encompasses a broad and diverse range of sexual and emotional desires, attractions, identities and relationships that exist outside of heterosexuality and traditional social norms. It frequently also includes those who are *gender diverse*, *asexual*, *aromantic* or simply not *cisgender* or heterosexual.

queerphobia. A broad range of prejudice, violence, fear, *microaggressions* and antagonism toward *queer* people. Queerphobia can be expressed through hateful rhetoric, incitements of violence, condemnation of queer people, demeaning jokes, vilifying statements, derisive comments and anti-LGBTQ+ political lobbying.

queerplatonic relationships. Committed intimate relationships that are not romantic in nature, but may include a sexual component in addition to emotional investment.

Many *aromantic* and *asexual* individuals prefer queer-platonic relationships to other partnered bonds.

rejection sensitivity dysphoria. The experience of severe sensitivity to or pain triggered by the perception of rejection, criticism or failing to meet others' standards and expectations.

relationship anarchy. An anarchic approach to relationships that rejects rules and expectations around intimate bonds, except for the ones that are mutually agreed upon by those within the relationships. A relationship anarchist is not incapable of commitment, but is open to adapting with the sometimes chaotic ebb and flow of connections, and is willing to radically adjust the structure of a relationship into something that works better if need be.

relationship escalator. The societal practice of finding committed monogamous companionship that follows a traditional structure of dating, moving in together, getting engaged, getting married, having kids and remaining together until death. Not everyone follows this path, and many *polyamorous* and *nonmonogamous* folks step off of the relationship escalator entirely as they formulate fulfilling bonds with multiple partners.

safer sex. Sexual activity in which an individual takes steps to protect their sexual health and wellness and that of their partners. Safer sex practices may include using condoms and barriers for penetrative and oral sex, regularly testing for sexually transmitted infections, not participating in one-night stands, requiring explicit consent from partners and establishing safe words in the bedroom.

sissy. A term that refers to an individual who enjoys being subjected to *sissification* or *feminization*.

sissification. A common *BDSM* exchange in which a *Dominant*, typically a *cis* woman, dresses a *submissive*, typically a cis man (referred to as a *sissy*), in hyperfeminine clothing, lingerie and makeup. The sissy is then sometimes made to do acts of servitude or is dominated sexually, including being penetrated with a strap-on or other toys. Also sometimes called *feminization*.

snowflakes. A demeaning term used by bigots and many conservatives to describe somebody they perceive as sensitive and weak. They frequently apply it in such a way to suggest that oppressed people, especially minorities, are looking for excuses to feel victimized, and that they just want to feel special and unique. It's a term that exists solely to belittle and dehumanize marginalized individuals who speak out about being discriminated against.

sub/submissive. The person who submits to a *Dominant* in a *BDSM* dynamic or scene.

t-dick. The bottom growth of the clitoris experienced by *trans* men and *trans masc* individuals who are taking testosterone.

TERF. An abbreviation for *trans* exclusive radical feminist. Refers to an ideological movement that does not accept trans women as real women, actively lobbies against *transgender* rights, strives to ban trans women from women's spaces, and even attempts to criminalize various aspects of being trans.

thirst pic. A picture taken with the intent to elicit an arousal response in others. Often more sexually suggestive than explicit.

tomboy. A term used to refer to girls or young women who present more masculine traits and styles of self-expression. Can also include those who engage in sports, or exhibit behaviours traditionally associated with boys.

trap. Somebody who takes pleasure in, and is excited by, subverting the expectations and assumptions that others have of their gender identity and expression.

trans. The short form of the word *transgender*.

transgender. An identity for somebody who identifies in any way as *gender diverse*, *gender nonconforming*, or otherwise not *cisgender*.

trans masc. A *trans* person who has a predominantly masculine gender identity and expression.

transmedicalism. The belief that being *trans* is a medical issue, and that somebody is not really *transgender* unless they experience severe gender *dysphoria* and actively seek medical or surgical transition. This harmful belief is often used to gatekeep, invalidate and demean *nonbinary* folks and trans individuals who choose not to medically or surgically transition. People who hold this belief are also known as transmed or truscum.

transphobia. A broad range of anti-trans sentiments, beliefs, opinions and fears often expressed through derision, dehumanization, ostracization, threats, intimidation and violence toward *trans*, *nonbinary* and *gender-diverse* people.

tube sites. Websites designed for uploading, hosting and streaming pornographic videos.

vaginoplasty. A surgical procedure performed to create or repair a vagina.

vasectomy. A form of birth control in which the tubes that carry sperm are cut or blocked so that sperm cannot reach the semen that is ejaculated from a person's body during orgasm. Some *trans* individuals consider this a gender-affirming minor surgery.

wokeness. A demeaning buzzword used by prejudiced individuals to describe anything that's progressive, forward thinking and inclusive of ethnicity, gender, sexuality or disability. Almost always followed by statements complaining about the visibility and inclusion of minorities in film, television and popular culture. It's lazy bigotry at its saddest.

RESOURCES

RELEVANT BOOKS

Barker, Meg-John, and Alex Iantaffi. *Life Isn't Binary: On Being Both, Beyond, and In Between.* Jessica Kingsley Publishers, 2019.

Beckett, Cooper S., and Lyndzi Miller. *The Pegging Book: A Complete Guide to Anal Sex with a Strap-On Dildo.* Thornapple Press, 2022.

Bergman, S. Bear, and Kate Bornstein, eds. *Gender Outlaws: The Next Generation.* Seal Press, 2010.

Bornstein, Kate. *Gender Outlaw: On Men, Women, and the Rest of Us.* Vintage, 2016.

Coyote, Ivan E. *Tomboy Survival Guide.* Arsenal Pulp Press, 2016.

Erickson-Schroth, Laura, ed. *Trans Bodies, Trans Selves: A Resource by and for Transgender Communities*, 2nd edition. Oxford University Press, 2022.

Fern, Jessica. *Polysecure: Attachment, Trauma and Consensual Nonmonogamy.* Thornapple Press, 2020.

Fern, Jessica, and David Cooley. *Polywise: A Deeper Dive into Navigating Open Relationships.* Thornapple Press, 2023.

Grimm, Bruce Owens, Miguel M. Morales and Tiff Joshua TJ Ferentini, eds. *Fat & Queer: An Anthology of Queer and Trans Bodies and Lives.* Jessica Kingsley Publishers, 2021.

Hill-Meyer, Tobi, ed. *Nerve Endings: The New Trans Erotic*. Instar Books, 2017.

Johnston, Alo. *Am I Trans Enough? How to Overcome Your Doubts and Find Your Authentic Self*. Jessica Kingsley Publishers, 2023.

Kobabe, Maia. *Gender Queer: A Memoir*. Oni Press, 2019.

Lore, Nillin, ed. *Heckin' Lewd: Trans and Nonbinary Erotica*. Bold Strokes Books, 2022.

Lorenz, Theo. *The Trans Self-Care Workbook: A Coloring Book and Journal for Trans and Non-Binary People*. Jessica Kingsley Publishers, 2020.

Notte, JoEllen. *In It Together: Navigating Depression with Partners, Friends, and Family*. Thornapple Press, 2023.

Notte, JoEllen. *The Monster Under the Bed: Sex, Depression, and the Conversations We Aren't Having*. Thornapple Press, 2020.

Patterson, Kevin A. *Love's Not Color Blind: Race and Representation in Polyamorous and Other Alternative Communities*. Thornapple Press, 2018.

Sawyers, Evita. *A Polyamory Devotional: 365 Daily Reflections for the Consensually Nonmonogamous*. Thornapple Press, 2023.

Sexsmith, Sinclair, ed. *Best Lesbian Erotica of the Year, Volume 4*. Cleis Press, 2019.

Sexsmith, Sinclair, ed. *Best Lesbian Erotica of the Year, Volume 5*. Cleis Press, 2020.

Sexsmith, Sinclair, ed. *Best Lesbian Erotica of the Year, Volume 6*. Cleis Press, 2022.

Sloan, Kate. *101 Kinky Things Even You Can Do*. Laurence King Publishing, 2021.

Sloan, Kate. *200 Words to Help You Talk about Sexuality and Gender*. Laurence King Publishing, 2022.

Sparks, Kelvin. *Trans Sex: A Guide for Adults*. Jessica Kingsley Publishers, 2022.

Spoon, Rae, and Ivan E. Coyote. *Gender Failures*. Arsenal Pulp Press, 2014.

Stryker, Kitty, ed. *Ask: Building Consent Culture*. Thornapple Press, 2017.

Tobia, Jacob. *Sissy: A Coming-of-Gender Story*. G. P. Putnam's Sons, 2019.

Violet, Mia. *Yes, You Are Trans Enough: My Transition from Self-Loathing to Self-Love*. Jessica Kingsley Publishers, 2019.

TRANS AND QUEER BLOGS

Girly Juice by Kate Sloan (she/her) (https://girlyjuice.net). Blog is sometimes NSFW. Kate Sloan is a bisexual, queer and demisexual writer, podcaster, journalist, singer and songwriter.

Jiz Lee by Jiz Lee (they/them) (https://jizlee.com). Blog is NSFW. A world-renowned nonbinary porn performer, advocate and activist.

Kelvin Sparks by Kelvin Sparks (they/them) (https://kelvinsparks.com). A trans masc sex blogger and writer who reviews sex toys and wrote an awesome trans-focused sex ed book.

Mx. Nillin by Nillin Lore (they/them) (https://mxnillin.
com). Blog is NSFW. It's me! Catalogues the past
decade of my intimate life as a chubby trans queer
and further explores mental health, self-worth,
trauma, sexuality and identity.

The Notice by Rae Chen (they/them) (https://thenotice.
net). A nonbinary, Canadian beauty blogger who
writes inclusive make-up guides and reviews lingerie
and sex toys.

On Queer Street by Quinn Rhodes (he/him) (https://
onqueerstreet.com). Blog is NSFW. A queer, trans and
disabled sex blogger who writes about sex, sexuality
and enthusiastic consent, while also exploring
himself as a sex nerd with vaginismus.

Quenby Creatives by Quenby Harley (they/them) (https://
quenbycreatives.com). A trans queer writer, activist
and performance artist, Harley is the creator of the
Trans Joy project and author of award-winning
queer smut.

Sugarbutch Chronicles by Sinclair Sexsmith (they/
them) (https://sugarbutch.net). A nonbinary writer of
queer erotica who also teaches about BDSM protocol
and dynamics through workshops, presentations
and posts.

TRANS QUEER-POSITIVE PORN

All of the following links are to websites designed for
adult-only audiences. This list is is far from exhaustive;
you can find tons of independent trans queer performers

and creatives making really outstanding sex- and body-positive smut on OnlyFans, Fansly and various social media platforms. It's well worth the effort to search key phrases (as described in chapter 8) and seek them out!

Aorta Films (https://aortafilms.com). Internationally award-winning indie queer porn.

Chelsea Submits (https://chelseasubmits.com). Queer trans lesbian porn star and Dutch American filmmaker Chelsea Poe was the winner of the 2015 Feminist Porn Award for "Hottest Trans Vignette." She's also a three-time Adult Video News Awards nominee for Transsexual Performer of the Year and an XBIZ Awards nominee for Transgender Performer of the Year.

Courtney Trouble (https://courtneytrouble.com). Queer filmmaker, photographer and promoter of trans indie porn.

The Crash Pad Series (https://crashpadseries.com). Diverse trans queer porn that features a broad range of identities, body types, ethnicities and disabilities in its talented and passionate performers.

FurAffinity (https://furaffinity.net). The internet's largest message board and social media platform for furries, artists and fursuiters. Has a very large trans and nonbinary queer community.

Murrtube (https://murrtube.net). Furry and pet play amateur porn streaming with predominantly trans queer content creators.

Pink Label TV (https://pinklabel.tv/on-demand/). A trans queer adult streaming platform that is home to over 100 LGBTQ+ adult film studios.

Trouble Films (https://troublefilms.com). Home of exclusive indie trans porn, dyke porn, BDSM and hardcore adult films and porn sites.

Vanniall (https://vanniall.com). An award-winning trans adult content creator, entertainer and sex worker who lives in New York City with her three black cats.

Yiffer (https://yiffer.xyz). A huge source of trans and queer furry sex comics, many of which are updated regularly as active works in progress.

INDEX

ALSO FROM THORNAPPLE PRESS

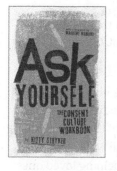

ASK YOURSELF: THE CONSENT CULTURE WORKBOOK

Kitty Stryker, with a foreword by Wagatwe Wanjuki

"*Ask: Building Consent Culture* editor Kitty Stryker invites readers to delve deeper, with guest experts and personal anecdotes, to manifest a culture of consent in one's own community that starts at the heart."

—Jiz Lee, editor of *Coming Out Like a Porn Star*

THE PEGGING BOOK: A COMPLETE GUIDE TO ANAL SEX WITH A STRAP-ON DILDO

Cooper S. Beckett and Lyndzi Miller

"Cooper and Lyndzi have created the smart, fun, accessible guide to pegging that we needed. Whether you are curious or already a pegging pro, this is a worthwhile addition to your sex ed book collection."

—JoEllen Notte, sex educator and author of *The Monster Under the Bed: Sex, Depression, and the Conversations We Aren't Having*

IN IT TOGETHER: NAVIGATING DEPRESSION WITH PARTNERS, FRIENDS, AND FAMILY

JoEllen Notte

"Am I allowed to say I laughed and had so much fun reading about depression? Read this book and you'll feel seen—and you'll walk away with a real-life guide to helping loved ones without sacrificing your own mental health."
—Meredith Goldstein, Boston Globe Love Letters advice columnist, podcast host and author of *Can't Help Myself*

MORE THAN TWO: CULTIVATING NONMONOGAMOUS RELATIONSHIPS WITH KINDNESS AND INTEGRITY

Eve Rickert with Andrea Zanin

Fully revised and updated second edition

A modern topology of nonmonogamy's many possibilities—and consequences.

ABOUT THE AUTHOR

Mx. Nillin Lore (they/them) is an AuDHD, nonbinary and queer activist, advocate and educator based in Saskatoon, Saskatchewan. They have had queer erotica stories published in a number of anthologies including *Best Lesbian Erotica of the Year* volumes 4–6 and *The Big Book of Orgasms Volume 2* (Cleis Press). They co-authored a chapter of *Trans Bodies, Trans Selves* (Oxford University Press) and are the editor of *Heckin' Lewd: Trans and Nonbinary Erotica*.

Photo courtesy of Evie Johnny Ruddy